1000 Amazing Horror Movie Facts

Tom Chapman

Contents

Introduction

Think you know all there is to know about horror movies? Well, think again. 1000 Amazing Horror Movie Facts is chock full of fascinating and unusual facts about classic (and not so classic) horror movies. Blockbusters, B-movies, slashers, ghost stories, video nasties, anthologies, sequels, gore, cursed productions, what might have been, casting, controversy, and so on. So dim the lights and prepare to enter the spooky and blood drenched world of horror movies....

The Facts

(1) It is sometimes suggested that Michael Myers in the Halloween films is based on the real life serial killer Edward Kemper. This is not true. John Carpenter based Michael Myers on a 'devil eyed' child he saw in a mental institution.

(2) The Texas Chainsaw Massacre was originally going to be called Head Cheese.

(3) The first film in the Saw franchise was shot in just 18 days.

(4) The story for Final Destination was originally proposed as an episode of The X-Files.

(5) 500 gallons of fake blood were used during production of the first Nightmare On Elm Street film.

(6) Special effects supervisor John Richardson, who staged the famous decapitation sequence in the 1976 film The Omen, was later involved in a car crash where his passenger, an assistant named Liz Moore, was decapitated for real. A sign near the accident marked the distance to a nearby town. It read - Ommen, 66.6 km.

(7) The serial killer Danny Harold Rolling, who became known as The Gainsville Ripper, was one of the inspirations for the Wes Craven movie Scream. Rolling had a habit of stalking and killing students.

(8) The Blair Witch Project cost only $60,000 to make but grossed $248.6 million.

(9) The famous theme song (by Lolita Ritmanis) to the Justice League cartoon is clearly stolen from the opening title music to the 1971 Hammer horror film Twins of Evil.

(10) John Landis made the early death of Griffin Dunne in An

American Werewolf in London as grisly and scary as possible to signal to audiences that this was a full blooded horror film - despite the sense of humour the movie patently has in spades.

(11) The production crew used real human skeletons in the 1982 film Poltergeist because they were cheaper to buy than realistic fake ones.

(12) The Bloody Benders are one of the inspirations for the Sawyer family in the Texas Chainsaw Massacre films. The Bloody Benders were a family of serial killers who lived in Labette County, Kansas. From 1871 to 1872 they are believed to have murdered around 20 people. The weird thing about the Bloody Benders is that the mother and daughter were a full part of the murders. Kate Bender, the daughter, would lure men to their house (which was a sort of general store) and Ma Bender would cook for them. While they were eating, the victims would be hit by a sledgehammer and have their throat cut. The motive for the murders was robbery. The Bloody Benders had their ruse uncovered when they killed a doctor. The brothers of the doctor organised a huge search for him in the area and the Bender home was searched. It was found to contain bodies which had been sent through a trapdoor. The locals burned down the Bender home. And the Bender family? They had vanished. No one really knows what happened to them.

(13) John Carpenter's The Thing was originally banned in Finland.

(14) The first Jack the Ripper film is believed to be The Lodger in 1926. This was Alfred Hitchcock's adaptation of the Marie Belloc Lowndes novel.

(15) Jaws is the scariest popcorn blockbuster ever made. The selection of the actress in the film to play Ellen Brody (the wife of the police chief played by Roy Scheider) was not exactly what you would call an open casting call. The producer on Jaws was Richard Zanuck and he promised the part of Ellen

Brody to his wife Linda Harrison. Harrison was famously the supermodel cavegirl Nova in the Planet of the Apes franchise. With the producer being her husband, Linda Harrison must have felt fairly confident that she had the part of Ellen Brody in the bag. She was to be disappointed though. The part of Ellen Brody was instead given to Lorraine Gary. Lorraine Gary was the wife of Sid Sheinberg and Sheinberg was the head of Universal. In this game of casting top trumps, the studio boss had pulled rank on the producer.

(16) The video game that Nick Frost's character Ed frequently plays in Shaun of the Dead is TimeSplitters 2.

(17) John Carpenter said he didn't want to direct The Thing because he loved the original and didn't care much for remakes. He had no choice though because it was the first time a studio had offered him a big film and he couldn't really turn it down.

(18) David Cronenberg turned down an offer to direct the Star Wars film Return of the Jedi in order to make his cult 1983 body horror film Videodrome.

(19) Shaun of the Dead cost $4 million to make and grossed $30 million.

(20) If you watch The Exorcist II: the Heretic, you might notice Dana Plato in a small role. Plato shot to fame at the age of 13 when she won a part in the hugely popular eighties sitcom Diff'rent Strokes. Plato had to choose between an ice-skating career and acting and, all things considered, she probably should have stuck with the ice-skating. Plato was booted off of Diff'rent Strokes for getting pregnant and her career went nowhere fast - thanks in large part to her drug problems. She lost custody of her son and ended up doing softcore erotic films to make ends meet. Plato even had breast augmentation in the hope of becoming a Playboy model. Plato was found dead in an RV in 1999. The verdict was an overdose of painkillers and other medication. She was just 34 years old.

Her money and fame was merely a distant memory by the time of her sad death.

(21) John Larroquette, who supplies the opening narration to The Texas Chainsaw Massacre, said years later that he'd never watched the film and never got paid for his contribution to it.

(22) The famous film critic Roger Ebert was critical of Jarlath Conroy's Irish accent in George Romero's Day of the Dead for not being very convincing. Unknown to Ebert though, Conroy is actually Irish in real life. That was his actual voice!

(23) The 1976 film The Town That Dreaded Sundown was based on a true crime case known as The Texarkana Moonlight Murders. The Texarkana Moonlight Murders featured an unknown killer who seemed to have stepped straight out of a real life horror film.

The murders took place in a sleepy town named Texarkana (between both Texas and Arkansas) in 1946. The murders took place three months apart and there were some attacks too where the victims survived. The first attack was on Jimmy Hollis, 24, and his girlfriend, Mary Jeanne Larey, 19. The victims were parked in a car in a quiet spot. The attacker wore what looked like a pillow case over his head with holes cut for his eyes. He brutally beat Jimmy with a pistol (fracturing his skull in the process) and sexually assaulted Mary Jeanne. Jimmy and Mary Jeane survived the attack but were left with traumatic memories of this awful incident. They were not killed because the lights from a passing car scared the attacker away.

A month later Richard Griffin, 29, and his girlfriend, Polly Ann Moore, 17, were shot dead in his car. Polly Ann Moore had been raped before she died. The police deduced that the victims had been shot outside the car and then put back in the car after their deaths. Three weeks later there was another shocking murder in the town. Fifteen year-old Betty Jo Booker and her friend Paul Brown were the victims. They had both been shot after stopping off close to a park. The killings were very brutal. Betty Jo had actually been shot in the face. She had also been raped. Her body was found some distance away from Paul Brown.

The police found that the same handgun had been used in both double-murders. This obviously meant that a serial killer was at large. Texarkana descended into panic at this latest double-murder. People began arming themselves and a curfew was put in place. Texarkana became the town that feared sundown. In May, a man named Virgil Starks was shot through his window while listening to the radio at home. His wife Katie was also shot as she tried to use the phone to get help. An intruder entered the house but Katie, despite her injuries, managed to escape and get to a nearby house. Was this the work of what had become known as The Phantom Slayer? It was possible although a different gun had been used this time. If this was the Phantom though it was to be the last attack. As for the police investigation, it was hobbled by the widely fluctuating alleged eyewitness accounts of the Phantom. The descriptions of the suspect were all over the place and not consistent. A college student confessed to the murders and then committed suicide but he was not believed to be the real killer.

The main suspect was Youell Swinney - a perennial car thief in the area. Swinney's wife told the police that he was the Phantom but then she retracted her story. As a consequence of this the police were never able to build a case against Swinney and find sufficient evidence to put him on trial. Swinney later ended up in prison for car theft. Those who believe he was the Phantom would point out that the killer never struck again once he was arrested. Swinney got out of prison in 1978 and died in 1994.

(24) Universal wanted Dan Aykroyd and John Belushi to play the leads in the classic John Landis film An American Werewolf in London.

(25) There are over fifty deadly traps in the Saw franchise.

(26) Prior to Sigourney Weaver being cast as female lead Ellen Ripley in Ridley Scott's Alien, the studio considered Kay Lenz, Meryl Streep, Helen Mirren, Genevieve Bujold, and Katherine Ross. Candice Bergen and Jane Fonda were both offered the part of Ripley but turned it down.

(27) The original concept for 1981's Halloween II was to have Michael Myers stalk Laurie Strode in a high rise tower.

(28) Stacy Keach was originally going to play Father Damien Karras in The Exorcist but they found Jason Miller and decided he would be a better fit for the character.

(29) The Wolf Creek horror films were based on Ivan Milat - a serial killer who murdered backpackers in the Australian outback. Milat was every bit as brutal and terrifying as Mick Taylor in the Wolf Creek films. Milat was the fifth of fourteen children born in Australia to Croatian immigrants. He was in and out of juvenile detention centres as a youngster and dangerously obsessed with knives and guns. His early crimes included theft, breaking and entering, and driving a stolen car. In 1971, Milat was charged with the abduction of two teenage hitchhikers - one of whom he raped. Milet fled to New Zealand in an attempt to evade the charges but was eventually arrested in 1974. However, the trial against him on kidnap charges collapsed.

He then got a job as a truck driver. This would turn out to be very bad news for some European backpackers. The victims of Milet were found in the Belanglo State Forest, 15 kilometres south-west of the New South Wales town of Berrima. Three were German and two were British. Milet even killed a couple of Australians. Milet would offer backpacking hitchhikers a lift in his truck and then restrain them at gunpoint. He would usually torture the victims before he killed them. One victim was stabbed 21 times in the chest and 19 times in the neck. Her spine had been severed. Another had been blindfolded, stabbed in the chest and then shot ten times. Milet was a terrifying man. He had a big Dennis Lilee mustache and an odiously creepy smile. He looked completely crazy. If you were backpacking in the outback miles from anywhere he was your worst nightmare. There was a huge police investigation when the bodies were discovered but it was a very difficult operation. Finding a killer in such a large area was literally like searching for a needle in a haystack. The crime scenes showed the victims had been sexually assaulted. There were also some bullet casings as the camp sites the killer had used. Milet would abduct the backpackers in pairs and then kill them separately. He genuinely seemed to love killing people and did so with sadistic relish.

The police managed to narrow the list of potential suspects down to 230 people but they then received some assistance from Paul Onions - a British backpacker who had escaped from Milet. Onions said that the man who offered him a lift and then pulled out a gun went by the name of Bill. He gave the police a description of 'Bill'. The police had further assistance from a former girlfriend of Milet who suggested him as a suspect. When the police searched Milet's home they found a large collection of knives and guns plus ammunition that matched evidence found at camp sites. They also found sleeping bags and clothes which they believed Milet had taken from the victims. The police also established that Milet had (suspiciously) sold his vehicle after the bodies were found and was not at work on any of the days when the victims were believed to have been abducted and killed.

This evidence, when stacked up, was all fairly conclusive. Milat was convicted of the murders on 27 July 1996 and was sentenced to seven consecutive life sentences. He died in prison in 2019 at the age of 74. Milet never confessed to any of the murders. Although no evidence has yet proven conclusive, it seems highly plausible that Ivan Milat killed more people than the Australian police are yet aware of.

(30) Gina Phillips was actually in her thirties when she played

a college student in the first Jeepers Creepers film.

(31) Wes Craven named Freddy Krueger after a bully who tormented him as a child.

(32) George Romero regretted making Barbara a largely catatonic and passive character in Night of the Living Dead. For the 1990 remake (which Romero wrote), he made Barbara much tougher.

(33) The blood washing away in the shower in Psycho after Janet Leigh's death was actually chocolate sauce. Because the film was in black and white it looked like blood.

(34) There are 60 different types of monster in the film The Cabin in the Woods.

(35) The Yankee Pedlar Inn in the 2012 horror film The Innkeepers is a real haunted hotel. The director (Ti West) of The Innkeepers had actually stayed in his hotel himself and experienced some strange incidents.

(36) Tony Todd had to put real bees in his mouth during the making of the film Candyman.

(37) Adrienne Barbeau is the voice of MacReady's computer chess game in John Carpenter's The Thing.

(38) The actors in Final Destination 3 had to ride the rollercoaster nearly 30 times for the premonition disaster sequence that opens the film.

(39) Scatman Crothers was made to do 85 takes by Stanley Kubrick shooting the scene in The Shining where he shows Wendy and Danny around the food storage areas of the Overlook Hotel.

(40) Tippi Hedren was 33 when she made The Birds for Alfred Hitchcock but the press releases pretended she was 28.

(41) Michael Caine turned down the part of Bob Rusk in Alfred Hitchcock's classic suspense thriller Frenzy because he thought both the part and the script was distasteful. The role was played by Barry Foster instead.

(42) A Nightmare On Elm Street was Johnny Depp's film debut. Depp attended auditions with his friend Jackie Earle Haley and was spotted by director Wes Craven. Haley later played Freddy in the 2010 remake.

(43) The name Ripley in the Alien franchise came from Ripley's Believe It Or Not. Ellen was the producer Walter Hill's mother's middle name - thus Ellen Ripley.

(44) Howling II: Your Sister Is a Werewolf is a famously terrible sequel to Joe Dante's werewolf film The Howling. Gary Brandner, the author of the novel on which the first film was based, hated Joe Dante because he felt Dante had ignored most of his book when he made the first film. Consequently, Dante was blocked from having the chance to make a sequel. The sequel was made on the cheap in Prague and directed by Philippe Mora - a mediocre filmmaker who made bad low-budget horror films his stock in trade. All you need to know about Howling II: Your Sister Is a Werewolf is that Christopher Lee had over 250 screen credits in his career and yet singled out this film as the worst one he'd ever appeared in.

Howling II: Your Sister Is a Werewolf doesn't have much to do with the first film. This is a very trashy and cheap looking film that seems to be more of a parody than anything else. It's rather boring though and relies a lot on Sybil Danning in very few clothes to get it through the lulls. Danning plays Stirba, an immortal werewolf queen. Much of the film takes place in dark gloomy settings and there is some god awful new wave music from a band in endless concert scenes. Christopher Lee looks dreadfully embarrassed to be here as the mysterious Stefan Crosscoe and - like the audience - seems to have no idea what is going on. One of the more remarkable things about the film is that they apparently sent the wrong costumes. Instead of werewolf costumes they were sent Planet of the Apes costumes instead and had to make do with them! So, instead of people looking like werewolves, they look like apes instead! It's one of but many things in Howling II: Your Sister Is a Werewolf that don't make much sense. This a terrible sequel that has little to do with the first film and is probably best avoided. Even fans of low-budget eighties horror are likely to have their patience stretched to breaking point by Howling II: Your Sister Is a Werewolf.

(45) Jason Vorhees was originally going to be called Josh. Josh Vorhees doesn't quite have the same ring does it?

(46) The Night Stalker, written by Richard Matheson, was a 1971 television film starring Darren Darren McGavin as a reporter named Cark Kolchak who stumbles into all manner of spooky goings on. It was fondly remembered by many (including Stephen King) and after an excellent sequel called The Night Strangler was later turned into a television series. Night Stalker probably visited the well too many times, becoming rather unrealistic in the end the way that Kolchak kept being drawn into a supernatural or monster themed investigation each week. He also had a knack of losing all of his evidence so no one ever believed him! The original television film though is regarded to be excellent.

(47) It's slightly odd that Freddy Krueger was a child killer who was murdered and now spends his time bumping off teenagers but ended up with a range of toy dolls and a young fanbase!

(48) The "Blair Monster" in the finale of John Carpenter's The Thing required 300 pounds of foam rubber.

(49) The Blair Witch Project was shot in just eight days.

(50) The skin masks and suits that Ed Gein fashioned from his graverobbing activities were the main inspiration for Leatherface in the Texas Chainsaw Massacre films. Gein's

unfathomable crimes spawned a number of films (sometimes loosely) based on his exploits - Psycho, The Silence of the Lambs, Deranged, In the Light of the Moon (which stars Steve Railsback as Gein). 1974's Deranged stars Roberts Blossom as Ezra Cobb (Cobb is clearly based on Gein), a nutty rural chap who exhumes his mother and begins abducting and killing local women. Deranged is a bit rough around the edges (it plainly didn't have much of a budget) but it's quite an effective little horror film. 2000's In the Light of the Moon is also worth watching. Although hardly a classic, In the Light of the Moon serves as a fairly accurate depiction of Ed Gein's crimes and is always fairly compelling. Ed Gein's unusual home decor and bone and skin themed bric-a-brac was also clearly a big influence on Texas Chainsaw Massacre. Yes, it's safe to say that Ed Gein has been a big inspiration when it comes to horror films.

(51) The original title for the first Final Destination film was Flight 180.

(52) Buffalo Bill in The Silence of the Lambs was partly based on Gary Heidnik. Heidnik was executed in 1999 for the murder, torture, and rape of six women in 1986 and 1987. He would keep the captives prisoner in a pit at the base of his house.

(53) The original concept for Joe Dante's Gremlins was more horrific. The gremlins were originally going to eat Billy's dog and kill his mother.

(54) Sam Raimi's The Evil Dead was banned in Germany until 2016.

(55) There have been over two hundred movies and television shows based on the work of Stephen King.

(56) The Texas Chainsaw Massacre cost less than $300,000 to make and eventually grossed $30 million in the U.S.

(57) There have been more films about Jack the Ripper than any other real life killer. The eclectic band of films and TV shows inspired by the Ripper includes A Study in Terror (an enjoyable 1965 film where Sherlock Holmes attempts to find the Ripper), Hammer's Hands of the Ripper, Murder by Decree (another film which blends fiction and fact by having Sherlock Holmes inhabit the same universe as the Ripper), and endless others - including an Italian-Spanish giallo film based on the notorious murderer. TV hows like Whitechapel and Ripper Street have been inspired by the case. Michael Caine starred in a decent (if TV santised) 1988 Jack the Ripper miniseries and the Ripper has even been transplanted to modern day America in silly films like Jack's Back. If you are interested in Jack the Ripper you must read Alan Moore's brilliant graphic novel From Hell if you haven't done so already. From Hell later inspired a terrible film adaptation with Johnny Depp.

(58) David Warner was the first choice to play Freddy Krueger in A Nightmare On Elm Street. Warner had done his Freddy make-up tests before a scheduling conflict emerged and he became unavailable - thus paving the way for Robert Englund to play the part.

(59) Danny Lloyd, who, as a child actor, played Danny Torrance in The Shining, said that he had no idea he was appearing in a horror film when he shot his scenes. Stanley Kubrick told him they were making a drama about a family who lives in a hotel.

(60) Bruce Campbell had some teeth knocked out while making the original Evil Dead when a cameraman slipped and hit him in the face with his camera.

(61) Duane Jones was the first black actor to play the lead hero in a horror film. This was in George Romero's classic 1968 film Night of the Living Dead. Despite the racial subtext of the film, Romero said Duane Jones was cast as the lead because he was the best affordable actor they knew and not because he was

black. Duane Jones was later director of the Maguire Theater at the State University of New York at Old Westbury and the artistic director of the Richard Allen Center for Culture and Art in Manhattan.

(62) The original 1958 version of The Fly, a big box-office hit of the era, was shot in just eighteen days.

(63) The 1973 film The Exorcist is one of the most famous horror movies ever made and was a huge blockbuster. The film made a (short lived) star of Linda Blair, who played Regan MacNeil - a twelve year old girl possessed by a demonic spirit. Warners Bros were understandably eager to make a sequel and it arrived in 1977 in the form of Exorcist II: The Heretic. With the acclaimed filmmaker John Boorman in the director's chair and Richard Burton in the cast what could possibly go wrong? Well, everything to be honest. Exorcist II: The Heretic is regarded to be one of the most disastrous sequels ever made.

The bizarre premise of Exorcist II: The Heretic has Regan MacNeil now 16 and living with a guardian in New York. Regan has suppressed the memories of the first film and is being treated at a high tech psychiatric institute. She is treated with a "synchronizer" - a device that merges brainwaves. Or something. The scenes of this in operation make the film look like a Gerry Anderson sci-fi show. Richard Burton plays a priest investigating the events of the first film. He naturally seeks out Regan. Exorcist II: The Heretic is a somewhat baffling film that was endlessly cut and re-edited - even as it hit cinemas. The film could not be salvaged though and got terrible reviews. It is just a very strange film full of bewildering creative decisions - like a scene where Linda Blair tapdances.

(64) Jenette Goldstein, who plays the trigger happy tomboy Vasquez in Aliens, turned up for her audition in a skirt and high heels as she had no idea what the film was about or who her character was.

(65) Seth Brundlefly's vomit in David Cronenberg's version of

The Fly was made from honey, eggs, and milk.

(66) Mia Farrow was tearfully on the brink of quitting the film Rosemary's Baby at one point to save her marriage to Frank Sinatra. With Rosemary's Baby falling behind schedule, Sinatra wanted her to quit to make a film called The Detective with him and warned the producer Robert Evans in phone calls that he better deliver her on time. To keep his star, Evans showed Farrow an hour of Rosemary's Baby and told her she was on course for an Oscar. A furious Sinatra then had divorce papers delivered on the set but Farrow had her revenge when Rosemary's Baby was a much bigger hit than Sinatra's film. Farrow even suggested to Evans they take out an ad contrasting the box-office figures.

(67) Paul Bateson was a former radiographer who appeared in the famous horror movie The Exorcist (during the hospital scene). Bateson was later a suspect in the case of a serial killer who was never captured. The 'bag murders' was the name given to a spate of killings in New York from 1975 to 1977. There were six murders in all. The victims were cut up before their remains were shoved in a bag and thrown in the Hudson River. As a consequence of this it was impossible to identify the victims and capturing the killer (who is generally known as The Greenwich Village Killer) proved equally complicated. The only lead the police had to go on was to place the clothing found on the remains under scrutiny. They managed to deduce that the victims seemed to be wearing items purchased from leather stores in Greenwich Village - specifically a fetish shop on Christopher Street. The location was a common haunt for the local gay community and so it seemed logical to presume that the victims were gay men.

While this all certainly narrowed down the lines of the investigation the inability to identify the victims was obviously a tremendous hindrance to the police. There was a suspect (of sorts) though in the end when it came to these harrowing murders. The suspect was Paul Bateson. Bateson seemed to fall on hard times after The Exorcist and began drinking a lot.

Things got so bad he ended up working in a porno cinema. Bateson was arrested in 1977 for the murder of a reporter named Addison Verrill. Verill covered the film scene for Variety and had been beaten and stabbed in his apartment. The police suspected at the time that it was a robbery and financially motivated. Bateson lived in Greenwich Village and frequented leather bars in the district. He was found guilty of Verrill's murder but during the trial the prosecution alleged that Bateson had confessed to other murders and said that he dismembered his victims and put them in bags. When one added all these details together then Bateson was a pretty strong suspect in the 'bag murders' investigation. The judge at the trial though dismissed the prosecution's attempt to portray Bateson as a serial killer and said the connections between the murder in question and other murders were too vague to be admissible.

Bateson was found guilty of the murder of Addison Verrill but (despite reports to the contrary) he has never confessed to being the person responsible for the bag murders and insists that he is innocent. Bateson apparently got out of prison in 2005. The police simply never had sufficient evidence to build a case against him for the bag murders. Sadly, because it was so long ago and the victims were impossible to identify the true identity of the killer may never be known. It could be that Bateson was The Greenwich Village Killer or it could have been someone else. The case of Paul Bateson loosely inspired the William Friedkin film Cruising. He was also depicted in the David Fincher television show Manhunter.

(68) Jason Statham was supposed to play Cooper in Neil Marshall's werewolf horror film Dog Soldiers but chose to make John Carpenter's Ghosts of Mars instead. Kevin McKidd replaced him.

(69) Dennis Radar was the inspiration for the Stephen King story A Good Marriage in his Full Dark, No Stars collection. This story was later turned into a forgettable movie. Radar became known as the BTK killer - BKT meaning bind, torture,

kill. Radar, who killed at least ten people, fitted security alarms for a living. He said many people had alarms fitted by him because of their fear of the BTK killer! Radar served in the Air Force as a young man and then got married before he worked in the security alarm business. Rader's family was sort of like the perfect disguise for a killer. Radar was the president of his local Christ Lutheran Church. He walked his daughter down the aisle when she got married. He was bald and wore glasses. You'd never suspect he was secretly a serial killer. He would usually strangle or suffocate (with a plastic bag) his victims. Sometimes he used a gun. One victim was stabbed though. Rader was very ruthless and killed families and children.

(70) The interiors of the hotel in Kubrick's The Shining don't make spatial sense and are designed to disorientate the viewer.

(71) Clive Barker was offered the chance to write and direct Alien 3 but he wasn't interested. Barker said his agent was absolutely furious and they soon parted company.

(72) The Amityville Horror is based on the alleged supernatural experiences of the Lutz family who bought a new home on 112 Ocean Avenue in Amityville, New York, a house where a mass murder had been committed the year before. After the family moved into their new house, they claimed a series of frightening paranormal events occurred. James Cromarty, who bought the house in 1977 and lived there with his wife Barbara for ten years, said - "Nothing weird ever happened, except for people coming by because of the book and the movie."

(73) Dominique Dunne portrayed Dana Freeling in the 1982 horror film Poltergeist. She had also been cast as Robin Maxwell in the television miniseries V (this popular miniseries was about seemingly humanoid and friendly aliens who come to Earth and turn out to be blood-drinking lizards who want to take over). Dunne was the sister of the actor Griffin Dunne. Her father was the famous journalist Dominick Dunne.

Around the time that V was in pre-production and about to start shooting in 1982, Dominique Dunne was 22 and in a relationship with a chef named John Sweeney. This relationship had become quite intense and Dominique Dunne decided she wanted to end it. Sweeney met Dominique Dunne in a residence they used to share and begged for her to give him another chance. She refused to do this and insisted that their relationship was over for good. Sweeney was so enraged by this that he throttled the actress for what was later determined to be at least four minutes in the driveway of the house. Dominique Dunne passed out and was put in a coma. She died in hospital for days later.

To the amazement of the family of Dominique Dunne, John Sweeney was convicted of voluntary manslaughter and only served three years in prison. It felt like a ludicrously light punishment for what appeared to be a case of murder. John Sweeney changed his name and tried to resume his career as a chef after his release. Dominique Dunne's family though hired private detectives to keep track of Sweeney and let any new employers or friends he found know who he really was. It would not bring back Dominique, but at the very least they were extracting some sort of revenge on Sweeney.

(74) Brandon Lee was the handsome son of the legendary Bruce Lee and began a promising career in Hollywood with action roles. Brandon's movies (Legacy of Rage, Laser Mission, Showdown in Little Tokyo, Rapid Fire) hadn't got great reviews but the critics were quite kind to him and said he was charismatic and likeable onscreen and had a good future in Hollywood. 1992's Rapid Fire was sort of like the first undiluted Brandon Lee film and suggested he could follow in the footsteps of people like Steven Seagal and Chuck Norris. Lee had an advantage over them too in that he looked a bit like Johnny Depp and was much younger. Brandon signed on next to appear in a film called The Crow - which was something of a departure. The Crow was a superhero film with horror elements and was considerably more ambitious than any film Brandon had been in before. Sadly, this would turn out to be

Brandon's last film. He was killed shooting The Crow when a live primer in a dummy round hit him at point blank range during a gun sequence. He was only 28 years-old.

The tragic accident happened on March 31, 1993. There were only eight days left on filming on the movie and Brandon was due to get married in the following few weeks when production on The Crow had concluded. The actor Michael Masse, who played a villain in The Crow, was part of a scene in which his character shot Brandon's character. When the stunt was concluded the crew became aware that Brandon was not moving. There was now a hole in his abdomen and he was rushed to hospital. Despite six hours of surgery he died of his injuries. The accident had occurred because the bullets used in the gun had been converted to blanks from live bullets. Blanks are supposed to have cardboard tips so that in the event of any accidental contact the damage is minimal. In this case though one of the lead tips from the modified live bullets was still in the gun and came loose during the scene - fatally hitting Brandon in the stomach. It was basically incompetence on the part of the people making the film.

The death was ruled an accident but Brandon's mother Linda Lee Cadwell launched a civil suit against the film studio - which was eventually settled out of court. The Crow turned out to be a pretty good film but this was obviously scant consolation to the late Brandon Lee and his distraught family. The Crow might well have made Brandon Lee a big star had he lived but - alas - we'll never know how his career would panned out now. The Crow was completed with the use of a double after Brandon's death. This was a rather spooky echo of how Bruce Lee's last film (Game of Death) was completed with a double after Bruce Lee died. It is sometimes said that Brandon fell victim to a family curse but this is patently fiction. The Crow was apparently quite an incompetent production and - sadly - it was safety issues on the set which cost Brandon Lee his life.

(75) JK Rowling says that some of the names in Harry Potter

were inspired by gravestones in Greyfriars Kirkyard - a graveyard she used to walk through in Edinburgh.

(76) Starship Troopers is a satirical science fiction horror action film directed by Paul Verhoeven and written by Edward Neumeier. It is based on a science fiction novel by Robert A Heinlein. This film tanked on its release but is now rightly regarded to be something of a classic. In the 23rd century Earth has taken on a distinctly fascist direction but propaganda assures everyone that they are living in a utopia. When humans encounter an insectoid species known as Arachnids (or "Bugs") they are soon plunged into a full scale war on the bug planet Klendathu. In this future Earth, military service is linked to citizenship and the military propaganda is amped up to the max as wholesome young recruits are sent into battle in the far reaches of space.

It's an incredibly subversive film given the huge studio budget. The raw recruits we follow at first are wide eyed and full of optimism. They are wholesome catalogue models who believe in citizenship and the flag. But what is basically happening is that they are being used as cannon fodder to fight an ill defined war for what is clearly an oppressive gung ho regime. The humans - not the bugs - are the REAL villains! Notice how Neil Patrick Harris as Colonel Jenkins is practically dressed like an SS officer by the end with a long leather trenchcoat. Verhoeven drew on Nazi propaganda films for inspiration. But here's the thing. The critics didn't understand the film when it was released and accused it of being fascist!

(77) Sigourney Weaver wore a bald cap for reshoots on Alien 3 because she refused to shave her head again.

(78) Lance Henriksen and Bill Paxton are the only actors to have been killed onscreen by a Xenomorph, Predator and Terminator.

(79) 1985's Return of the Living Dead was directed by Dan O'Bannon. The film has its roots in a novel by John Russo also

called Return of the Living Dead. When Russo and George A Romero parted ways after their 1968 film Night of the Living Dead, Russo retained the rights to any titles featuring 'Living Dead' while Romero was free to create his own series of sequels, beginning with Dawn of the Dead.

(80) Sam Raimi has said he now regrets the 'tree rape' scene in The Evil Dead.

(81) Peter Cushing was absent from an Amicus anthology for the first time in Vault of Horror as he was busy filming And Now the Screaming Starts! - also an Amicus film.

(82) The actor who plays the wheelchair bound Franklyn in The Texas Chainsaw Massacre was encouraged to method act by Tobe Hooper. As a consequence of this he never changed his clothes and was pedantic and whiney offscreen. This obviously didn't endear him to the other actors.

(83) Tales from the Darkside: The Movie was originally supposed to be Creepshow 3 but ended up becoming a movie of the TV show Tales from the Darkside.

(84) A brilliant 1995 film called The Young Poisoner's Handbook was based on Graham Young. Graham Young was known as The Teacup Poisoner. He was sent to Broadmoor in 1962 for poisoning his family and killing his stepmother. Deemed cured, he was released nine years later and secured work at a laboratory. Soon, the work colleagues of Young began to fall mysteriously ill. He had of course been poisoning them as part of his chemical experiments! Young was arrested in 1971 and found to have dangerous chemicals on him. He was sentenced to life in prison and died in 1990. Young killed at least three people (the true tally is probably higher) and made many more terribly ill. He was found to have kept a detailed diary of his experiments. The version of Young depicted in the 1995 film though is more likeable than the real person. The real Graham Young was said to be obsessed with Nazis and became friends with the Moors Murderer Ian Brady

at Broadmoor.

(85) Steve McQueen plays a high school student in the 1958 film The Blob despite the fact that he was nearly 30 at the time.

(86) The premature deaths of child actor Heather O'Rourke (who died of cardiac-pulmonary arrest and septic shock) and fellow Poltergeist cast member Dominique Dunne (who was strangled by her boyfriend when she was only 22) have led to theories of a 'Poltergeist Curse' but these deaths seem more like random and awful tragedies than anything. JoBeth Williams, Craig T. Nelson, and Oliver Robins, who played the other members of the Freeling family in Poltergeist, are all still very much alive and would appear to rebuff any claims about a supernatural jinx. Other evidence for the alleged curse involves Julian Beck, who starred as Kane in Poltergeist II: The Other Side, dying of stomach cancer months before the film even came out in theatres and Will Sampson, the actor who performed the exorcism, dying of malnutrition and postoperative kidney failure at age 53. In 2009, Lou Perryman, who played Pugsley in the original film, was murdered in his own home by an ex-convict with an axe.

(87) The first Hellraiser film was made in England but the studio New Line later decided they wanted it to be set in America. To this end, they dubbed some American accents into the film and pretended it was set in America - which it clearly isn't. Clive Barker made light of this on the audio commentary. As he notes, you can clearly see a very British train go past at one point!

(88) Suzanna Leigh, who starred in Hammer's Lust for a Vampire and the Amicus film The Deadly Bees, appeared in a film with Elvis and remained friends with him until his death.

(89) Stanley Kubrick was offered the chance to direct The Exorcist but he wasn't interested.

(90) The first actor to play the notorious serial killer Ted Bundy was Mark Harmon in the 1986 NBC television film The Deliberate Stranger. The actor Robert Hays (who you might know from the Airplane! comedy spoof films) was originally asked to play Ted Bundy in The Deliberate Stranger but felt it was a distasteful project and wanted no part of it. The Deliberate Stranger is very good on the whole - though of course diluted for television (you won't get to see too much of Bundy killing anyone). What the film does well is show us how Bundy (with his plaster of paris ruse where he would pretend to have a broken arm and ask women to help carry his library books to his car) could be quite charming. He managed to lull victims into a false sense of security.

(91) George A Romero got the idea for Dawn of the Dead when he was given a tour of a shopping mall in Monroeville, a few miles from downtown Pittsburgh. Shooting the film at the mall was difficult and meant most of the production took place at night. Each morning, as the Dawn of the Dead crew packed up to leave, a large group of senior citizens would arrive at the mall for an exercise class. The senior citizens would often be greeted by extras made up as zombies!

(92) The classic Alfred Hitchcock film Frenzy was heavily inspired by the Jack the Stripper murders. Hammersmith in London was the scene of a number of grisly murders in 1964 and 1965. The killer became known as Jack the Stripper because the murder victims were all prostitutes and always had their clothes and belongings (including, believe it or not, false teeth) removed. However, despite a huge police operation, the killer was never found and the murders remain a mystery to this day. The puzzling thing about the murders is that none of the victims displayed any evidence of sexual violence. The police detective heading up the search for Jack the Stripper in the 1960s predicted that the case would be as famous as the Jack the Ripper murders. He was obviously completely wrong about that. A lot of people today seem to have barely heard of Jack the Stripper.

(93) The camera pan across the misty pond in The Evil Dead was done by director Sam Raimi being pushed in a dinghy.

(94) Quatermass author Nigel Kneale worked on the screenplay for Halloween III but asked for his name to be taken off the credits because he didn't like the gore added to the film.

(95) Brian Dennehy almost played the doctor in John Carpenter's The Thing but Richard Dysart won the part in the end.

(96) Anthony Perkins said that Alfred Hitchcock was very distraught by a Psycho preview screening where people were openly laughing at the film.

(97) Tobe Hooper said he got the idea for The Texas Chainsaw Massacre when he was shopping in a store and noticed a rack of chainsaws for sale.

(98) The jigsaw puppet in Saw was made from scratch by the filmmakers.

(99) The Deadly Spawn is a 1983 horror film directed by Douglas McKeown. The film was sometimes known as Return of the Aliens: The Deadly Spawn or The Return of the Alien's Deadly Spawn - to cash in on Ridley Scott's Alien. This is a very low-budget horror film made over weekends but it has become mildly cultish mainly thanks to the gruesome special effects. The basic plot has a meteorite crashing in some woods, releasing man eating slug creatures which grow very quickly. Some of these creatures take residence in the basement of a family home and horror soon abounds when it starts eating anyone who ventures down there. The Deadly Spawn is a likeable enough bargain basement horror, sort of like a more bloody version of Critters or Tremors. The main alien monster is a rubbery looking monster with a large mouth full of fangs and certainly owes something (if not everything) to Giger's alien. This is one of the less copycat Alien inspired films as it

takes place in a family home but you can sort of see some similarities. Although the monster scenes have some enjoyably bloody deaths you do have to sit through a few dull patches featuring some highly variable acting from the no name cast (who, to be fair to them, were acting in what was essentially a home movie of sorts given its modest budget and shooting schedule). The Deadly Spawn is decent fun for those who like eighties horror and the soundtrack is enjoyable too.

(100) The music score for John Carpenter's Halloween was inspired by Dario Argento's Suspiria and Tubular Bells from The Exorcist.

(101) Malta born Mary and Madeleine Collinson are famous as the twin sisters in the cultish Twins of Evil with Peter Cushing. They were Playboy Playmates of the month in October 1970 - which would explain how they got in the film. They said the reason they didn't have much of an acting career after 1971 is that they only wanted to work together and most films obviously don't have any need of twins as characters.

(102) 1985's Lifeforce was Tobe Hooper's first film in his Cannon Films contract and had a $25 million budget. It practically bankrupted the studio when it failed at the box-office. Though we think of Cannon as a somewhat bargain basement studio, Tobe Hooper had a bigger budget on Lifeforce than he did on Poltergeist with Steven Spielberg.

(103) Robert Aldrich, director of Whatever Happened To Baby Jane and The Dirty Dozen, was the original choice to direct Alien. The ideas of Aldrich didn't quite mesh with those of the producers though - thus eventually paving the way for Ridley Scott to make the film.

(104) John Carpenter was supposed to direct Halloween H20: 20 Years Later but he left the project because of a disagreement with the producer Moustapha Akkad over his fee.

(105) Michael Reilly Burke was the second actor to portray Ted Bundy. He played Bundy in the 2002 Matthew Bright film Ted Bundy. This second Bundy film is not bad but never quite distinguishes itself or ever really justifies its existence. The film plays rather loose with the Bundy story and Burke also seems a little over the top at times. You could believe that Mark Harmon's Bundy could hide in plain sight all the time but you don't get that sense with the depiction of Bundy by Michael Reilly Burke. The film is rather silly at times - especially in the sequence where Bundy goes to the electric chair.

(106) The Shining is in the Guinness Book of Records for the most retakes of a single scene with 127 takes for a scene with Shelley Duvall.

(107) Return of the Living Dead was originally going to be a 3D film directed by Tobe Hooper.

(108) Marilyn Burns had so much fake blood on her during the production of The Texas Chainsaw Massacre that her clothes were almost solid by the end of the shoot.

(109) 9,500 'Babadook Pop-Up Books' were hand created and sold.

(110) The sequel Aliens v Predator: Requiem got terrible reviews and wrecked any chance of further Alien v Predator films. One of the biggest complaints was that the film was so dimly lit you couldn't actually see what was happening half of the time!

(111) The opening sweeping shots of the countryside in Kubrick's The Shining were used in Blade Runner's original theatrical ending.

(112) Cary Grant and Sean Connery were considered for the part of Mitch Brenner in The Birds.

(113) The original ending of George Romero's Dawn of the Dead was supposed to have Peter and Fran commit suicide but - after some consideration - it was considered too bleak.

(114) Vincent Price said that he didn't like the 1986 remake of The Fly because it was too explicit when it came to gore and blood. Price felt that a film of this type worked better when it was more suggestive.

(115) Three actors from the original Dawn of the Dead have cameos in Zack Synder's 2004 remake. Appearing on the television the survivors watch is Ken Foree (who played Peter from the original). He plays an evangelist who asserts that God is punishing mankind. Scott H. Reiniger, who played Roger in the original, plays an army general telling everyone to stay at home for safety. Tom Savini, who did the special effects for many of Romero's films and played the motorcycle gang member Blades in the original Dawn of the Dead, plays the Monroeville Sheriff.

(116) The opening sequence of John Carpenter's Halloween is inspired by the opening sequence of Orson Welles' Touch of Evil.

(117) The famous eyeball gulping scene in Evil Dead II was shot in reverse.

(118) Anthony Perkins was something of a heart-throb before Psycho and had even released a music album. The film rather typecast him though and he invariably had to play odd and eccentric characters thereafter.

(119) George Romero said he didn't like zombie films where the zombies can run. He thought zombies were scarier if they slowly shuffled around and crept up on you.

(120) A producer on Return of the Living Dead was not happy when he visited the set and saw Linnea Quigley was nude for her strip tease graveyard scene. The producer made them tone

down the scene.

(121) Shaun works at 'Foree Electric' in Shaun of the Dead. This is a reference to Dawn of the Dead star Ken Foree.

(122) Jack Nicholson declined the role of Father Lamont in The Exorcist II. That was clearly a shrewd decision.

(123) Predator 2 required 20 cuts to get an R rating.

(124) Christopher Lee turned down the role of Dr Loomis in John Carpenter's Halloween. The part was played by Donald Pleasance instead. Lee later said he regretted turning down this role.

(125) Melissa Joan Hart, Brittany Murphy, Alicia Witt, Melanie Lynskey and Melinda Clarke were all considered for the part played by Neve Campbell in Wes Craven's Scream.

(126) The studio wanted Marlon Brando to play Father Lankester Merrin in The Exorcist. They obviously didn't get their way on this.

(127) Beyond the Black Rainbow is a rather obscure Canadian science fiction horror film written and directed by Panos Cosmatos. Beyond the Black Rainbow is set in 1983 and takes place at a research facility called the Arboria Institute. The facility is investigating the mind and its connection to science and stimuli. They seek to explore sensory therapy in a new age of enlightenment. Dr Barry Nyle (Michael Rogers) seems to be one of the few scientists left in the facility and is keeping a young woman named Elena (Eva Allan) captive in the depths of the laboratory. Elena has psychic powers and communicates through telepathy. She eventually tries to escape. Beyond the Black Rainbow is a bizarre film and an enjoyably surreal experience.

Several years later when Stranger Things became a huge success, film buffs who had watched Beyond the Black

Rainbow noticed some interesting similarities between Stranger Things and this little known movie. Both are set in 1983. The telepathic girl's name (Elena) is close to Eleven. After she escapes from the lab, Elena nervously explores in the woods just as Eleven does in the first episode of Stranger Things. Beyond the Black Rainbow also has a synth music score that sounds similar to the one in Stranger Things. There is even a 'vat' scene in Beyond the Black Rainbow that unavoidably reminds one of the sensory deprivation tank in Stranger Things. Both Elena and Eleven kill their captors with mind powers and television (as a means of entertainment and vessel of communication) is vital to both characters. Dr Barry Nyle is rather similar to Matthew Modine's Dr Brenner in both his treatment of and fascination with his telepathic subject. As an experience in its own right though, Beyond the Black Rainbow is beautifully strange and full of incredible imagery. This is rather like some strange unknown science fiction film that you'd find in an eighties video store.

Beyond the Black Rainbow is not the most coherent film you'll ever watch but it is a rewarding and interesting experience. If you love Stranger Things, watch Beyond the Black Rainbow and see what you think of all the alleged similarities.

(128) It took two days for Robert Shaw to complete the USS Indianapolis speech in Jaws because he was drunk the first time he did it.

(129) The 2006 horror thriller Hard Candy was shot in just eighteen days.

(130) Casting Regan MacNeil, the twelve year old girl possessed by the devil in The Exorcist, was not easy. 600 child actors were considered before they found Linda Blair. Blair seemed very natural and intelligent to the director William Friedkin. She had even read the book the film was based on.

(131) Psycho was a taboo breaking film in many ways, not just for the violent end of Marion but also the scenes of Janet Leigh

and John Gavin in the bedroom depicting their affair. This was deemed to be incredibly bold at the time.

(132) Swedish actress Noomi Rapace beat Natalie Portman to win the role of the female lead Elizabeth Shaw in Prometheus.

(133) The Collector is a 1965 psychological thriller film based on the compelling 1963 novel by John Fowles. It was directed by William Wyler. Frederick Clegg (Terence Stamp) collects butterflies and takes photographs in his spare time but is completely detached from society and both socially awkward and shy. Clegg purchases a remote cottage and becomes obsessed with an art student called Miranda Grey (Samantha Aggar). After carefully observing Miranda for a time, Clegg kidnaps her with the aid of chloroform and imprisons her in the cellar of his remote cottage - which he has carefully prepared for the latest addition to his 'collection'. Clegg promises not to harm or abuse Miranda and believes that if he can keep her there and shower her with gifts she will come to love him and agree to stay for good. This story was a big influence on Stephen King's Misery.

(134) Alien 3 is the first Alien film to use some CGI to depict the alien.

(135) Society is a 1989 American body horror film directed by Brian Yuzna. Society concerns a teenager named Bill who lives a comfortable life with his family in Beverly Hills, California. For reasons he can't quite pinpoint though, Bill doesn't trust his family and feels like an outsider. His instincts prove to be horribly on the mark when the real truth about his relatives comes to light. Society is a social satire for much of its running time but the last act has a stomach churning twist that comes in the form of some truly unforgettable special effects. You definitely won't forget the last act of this film in a hurry.

(136) Saw seems to owe something to the Canadian horror film Cube - which features a group of people who awake to find they've been imprisoned in a giant cube and must escape from

some deadly booby traps.

(137) You can pinpoint where the film and the directors of
Alien v Predator: Requiem have completely given up because
they start making Ripley lookalike Reiko Aylesworth pose with
a Newtesque child and start using riffs from James Horner's
Aliens score. There's even a rip-off of the APC from Aliens. It's
such a self defeating direction to go in. Why remind us of
Aliens? All you are doing is reminding us of how much better
that film is!

(138) Eileen Dietz was the double for Linda Blair on The
Exorcist. She did the scenes which were considered too
extreme for a child actress - like for example the crucifix scene.

(139) Lord of the Flies was published 1954 and has influenced
everything from Battle Royale, to Lost, to The Hunger Games..
Most people will be familiar with the plot of this classic novel
by now. A group of British schoolboys are involved in a plane
crash and find themselves stranded on a remote island in the
Pacific Ocean with no adult supervision. How will they react to
this precarious situation? Well, not very well in some cases as
a battle between society and barbarism soon entails.

The influence of Lord of the Flies can still be felt in Young
Adult fiction and popular culture of the modern era. Battle
Royale is clearly influenced by Lord of the Flies as was the
popular television show Lost. One can see the influence of
Lord of the Flies on The Hunger Games too. The inspiration of
William Golding to write Lord of the Flies was that he noticed
how children in books were frequently depicted as sweet or
harmless. It struck him that this was not necessarily a realistic
depiction of childhood. What if you put children in a world
where there were no adults and they had to make up the rules
for themselves? That could be a recipe for disaster. Would the
children turn on one another? Would they retreat into
primitive behaviour?

It is debatable how realistic Lord of the Flies is (there have actually been cases of children becoming stranded on an island in real life and managing to work together and maintain friendly relations) but there is no denying that this is a thrilling adventure novel with a social subtext and elements of horror. You will be genuinely gripped the further you get into the story and the tropical island serves as an unforgettable backdrop for the drama to take place. Lord of the Flies, more than anything, is about the need to remain civilised - even in the most dire of circumstances. If humanity loses its ability to be civilised then there is no hope for any of us no matter if we are children or adults. Lord of the Flies is deserving of its status as a cult novel and its influence on the world of fiction (both on the page and on the screen) continues to be strongly felt today. The 1963 film version of this novel is well worth watching.

(140) Orphan is a 2009 psychological horror film directed by Jaume Collet-Serra and written by David Leslie Johnson from a story by Alex Mace. The premise concerns a couple who, after the death of their unborn child, adopt a mysterious nine year-old girl from Russia. The film drew mixed reviews and was a moderate hit - making $78 million from a $20 million budget. The plot of the film was felt by many critics to be far-fetched but it was actually based on a real life event in the Czech Republic which is generally known as the Kurim case in true crime circles.

(141) Scenes of Sissy Spacek destroying petrol stations in Carrie were scrapped because they would have been too expensive to film.

(142) Damien Thorn in the Omen films was originally going to be called Domlin Thorn.

(143) Betsy Palmer said she only took the role of Pamela Voorhees in Friday the 13th because she was broke and needed a new car.

(144) James DeMonaco said he got the idea for The Purge

from a road rage incident.

(145) The real life killer Albert Fish is considered to have been one of the inspirations for Hannibal Lecter.

(146) Troll 2 is a famously awful film that was produced under the title Goblins. A name change was undertaken to position it as a sequel to the 1986 film Troll although it has scant connection to that earlier picture. The plot of this nonsense has a family moving to a farming area where it turns out that vegetarian Goblins abound. The Goblins turn people into plants and then eat you. Or something like that. Troll 2 is a popular clip treasure trove on Youtube for its terrible acting and bizarre incoherence. The cast look as if they've never acted in their life and deliver comical line readings as they try their best to play out this preposterous material. This is the sort of film that Mystery Science Theater 3000 was invented for.

(147) Amicus were best known for their enjoyable sixties and seventies anthology horror films. The founders Milton Subotsky and Max J Rosenberg were Americans and based Amicus at Shepperton Studios. They were very shrewd in managing to entice some big names (admittedly some of whom were on the way down) into their films and keeping costs down. The contemporary settings of the horror compendiums were a clever way to save cash by not having to recreate period settings with costumes and sets.

(149) The Purge TV show was called American Nightmare in France.

(150) Hausu (House) was the first full-length film of Obayashi Nobuhiko. This surreal 1977 Japanese horror film is one of the most idiosyncratic movies you are ever likely to encounter. The plot, such as it is, concerns some schoolgirls - Gorgeous (Kimiko Ikegami), Fantasy (Oba Kumiko), Sweet (Miyako Masayo), Melody (Tanaka Eriko), Kung Fu (Jinbo Miki), Prof (Matsubara Ai) and Mac (Satô Mieko) - going to the country to stay with the aunt of Gorgeous. Once they arrive, strange

happenings begin to abound and that would be putting it mildly. There's a demon cat, a killer piano, deadly futons, and more surreal carnage than you can possibly imagine. Hausu is a famously bonkers film but it might be a brilliant one too. This is rather in the vein of cinema like the Monkees film Head or The Rocky Horror Picture Show - only much stranger and given a haunted house premise. Nothing in this film makes any sense and yet that's one of the joys. Upbeat pop music plays throughout and there are dizzying camera angles and captivating backwards and slow motion shots. Sometimes the backdrops become cartoons and the whole effect is so bizarre and inventive that you just go with the flow and embrace this joyfully offbeat piece of cinema.

The film uses all manner of special effects including what look like picture 'cut-outs' and is a remarkable feat of filmmaking. The random shifts of tone are very eccentric and very enjoyable as a consequence. No few minutes of this film are ever the same and the insane collage of flashback, drama, comedy, horror, kung fu, becomes completely entrancing. Obayashi Nobuhiko has a filmmaking style that makes Edgar Wright look like Ken Loach. Hausu is like an LSD trip that has been captured on film. The acting is nothing amazing but then that's not really the point of the film. There are some subtexts in the film that seem to be about war and devastation (something which would clearly be something that those of Nobuhiko's generation still felt most vividly) but to look for a narrative structure or deep meaning to Hausu is probably to miss the point. This is a film where one simply has to go with the flow and enjoy all of the eccentricity and incredible imagery that is thrown our way. Hausu is a remarkable experience and not to be missed for anyone who enjoys the stranger side of cinema.

(151) Chloë Grace Moretz was set to play Beverly Marsh in the film version of Stephen King's IT but the film took so long to go into production that Moretz was too old by the time the cameras rolled. Sophia Lillis played the part in the end.

(152) The Texas Chainsaw Massacre 2 was banned in Australia for 20 years.

(153) You might wonder why you don't see Alison Lohman, the star of Sam Raimi's Drag Me to Hell, in anything these days. That's because Lohman retired from acting so she could spend more time with her children.

(154) Dan O'Bannon said it is just a coincidence that there are characters named Bert and Ernie in Return of the Living Dead.

(155) Vincent Price turned down the part played by Roddy McDowall in Fright Night.

(156) Although it was the best reviewed of the Elm Street sequels, Wes Craven's New Nightmare was the least successful at the box-office.

(157) The ape village in the original Planet of the Apes film is modelled on the work of legendary Spanish architect Antoni Gaudí and the Göreme Valley in Cappadocia, Turkey.

(158) Nicholas Cage auditioned for the part of villain Buddy Repperton in John Carpenter's Christine.

(159) Clint Eastwood was offered the role played by Mel Gibson in the M. Night Shyamalan film Signs.

(160) In the original script for 28 Days Later the characters were going to end up in the lab where the virus broke out in order to try and find a cure. This was scrapped and replaced by a new plot involving the squad of soldiers at the country mansion.

(161) The role of Lieutenant Mike Harrigan in Predator 2 was played by Danny Glover. However, the first choice for this part was Patrick Swayze. Swayze could not do Predator 2 though because he had injured himself on another film and needed a break from action movies in order to heal.

(162) Child's Play 3 was banned in Britain from 1993 to 2002 after it was preposterously implicated in the tragic murder of a child named James Bulger by two boys.

(163) Veronica Cartwright played Lambert in the classic Ridley Scott sci-fi horror film Alien. However, Cartwright said she turned up to shoot the film under the impression that she was playing Ripley (the role that made Sigourney Weaver a star). Veronica Cartwright was furious to find herself relegated to the role of Lambert and made no attempt to hide her displeasure. She believes that most of Lambert's scenes in the theatrical cut of Alien were deliberately left on the cutting room floor as a punishment for her griping. "I had only read for Ripley," said Cartwright, "and when I got over to England they called up and said, 'Can you go in for wardrobe for Lambert?' I went, 'Oh no, I'm Ripley.' I had to call my agent and he said, 'No, you're Ripley.' It was so bizarre and so I had to re-read the script from the point of view of Lambert, and I thought she was a bit of a whiny bitch, but I think she became the voice of the audience; she was the only sane character, if you think about it. Nobody said anything. I guess I must have misunderstood. I brought it up a couple of times. If you've ever seen the big box set (DVD of Alien) there are nine outtakes and I'm in eight of them. I had a big part in that movie and it was changed."

(164) The Conjuring was originally going to quietly open at the start of the year but after positive test screenings the studio held it back for a bigger summer release.

(165) Creepycatalog.com ranked Peter Jackson's 1992 film Braindead as the goriest film ever made.

(166) A film was actually made about the necrophile serial killer Dennis Nilsen in 1989 called Cold Light of Day. However, the film is so low-budget and amateurish that it was quickly forgotten. Cold Light of Day was directed by Fhiona-Louise and features Bob Flag as Nilsen (called Jordan March

in the film although it is clearly based on Nilsen). The film is a rather grim experience. It shows Nilsen/March strangling people and boiling heads.

(167) A number of studios refused to make Psycho but it became Hitchcock's most successful film and grossed $32 million.

(168) Tony Todd said he was stung by bees 26 times over the course of making the Candyman trilogy.

(169) Jamie Bell was originally cast as Columbus in Zombieland but had to drop out due to other commitments.

(170) Tommy Lee Jones turned down the part of the android Ash in Alien.

(171) Doug Bradley's make-up to play Pinhead in Hellraiser took about six hours to apply.

(172) Al Matthews, who plays Sergeant Apone in Aliens, was a real life army veteran.

(173) Mel Brooks was the producer on David Cronenberg's remake of The Fly. Brooks kept his name off a lot of the promotional material lest people should think the movie was a comedy.

(174) The found footage monster film Cloverfield made inventive use of (the now largely defunct) social media site Myspace in its promotional campaign.

(175) Gene Hackman held the rights to The Silence of the Lambs at one point and planned to both direct and star in the film. He is believed to have got cold feet though due to the violence and darkness the film would unavoidably contain.

(176) Sean S. Cunningham began promoting the original Friday the 13th film before he even had a script. It evidently

worked as he secured funding on the concept and title alone.

(177) Jessica Harper turned down a part in Woody Allen's Annie Hall to star in the classic horror movie Suspiria.

(178) The 1980 cultish favourite Motel Hell was shot in just five weeks.

(179) In the film version of Blade with Wesley Snipes, the character is from Detroit. In the original comics though the character is from London.

(180) Winona Ryder had a panic attack shooting the underwater sequence in Alien Resurrection because of a childhood incident where she nearly drowned.

(181) A planned scene that didn't appear in The Texas Chainsaw Massacre 2 had Leatherface laying waste to a bunch of football fans in a parking lot. You can see a rough cut of this sequence online if you look for it. Tobe Hooper said the second unit director messed up this sequence so it was never really finished.

(182) Tales from the Hood is an underrated 1995 horror anthology directed by Rusty Cundieff. This was produced by Spike Lee and gives you four stories of urban horror that touch on themes like racism and gang culture.

(183) When she appeared in Psycho II, Meg Tilly had never seen the original Psycho. She said she wasn't allowed to watch television growing up so had never encountered the film before. Tilly said that making this film was rough as Perkins and the director Richard Franklin were very difficult people to work with.

(184) Omen III: The Final Conflict was called Barbara's Baby in Germany in a doomed attempt to latch onto the famed horror film Rosemary's Baby.

(185) Despite playing the bullied put upon Carrie, Sissy Spacek was actually a Prom queen in her own school days.

(186) Alien Resurrection was the first Alien film not to be made in England.

(187) The story for Scream 2 had to be altered when a draft of the script leaked online.

(188) The child actor Heather O'Rourke sadly died before Poltergeist III was released. Heather died while Poltergeist III was in post-production. Some reshoots were required to change the ending and so an eleven year-old child actor named Heather Holty had to stand in as Heather's character Carol Anne Freeling. The director Gary Sherman didn't want to finish the film after Heather's death but studio pressure apparently forced him to complete it. Poltergeist III received poor reviews and was a box-office flop.

(189) Peter Cushing and Christopher Lee become friends and frequent co-stars after appearing in the Hammer film The Curse of Frankenstein.

(190) Camille Keaton, the star of I Spit on Your Grave, is the grand-niece of the legendary comedian Buster Keaton.

(191) Jaws 2 was the first Hollywood film sequel to use '2' instead of Roman numerals.

(192) David's werewolf transformation scene in An American Werewolf in London took six days to shoot.

(193) The notorious Wes Craven film The Last House on the Left is inspired by Ingmar Bergman's The Virgin Spring.

(194) Freddy Krueger kills around fifty people in the Nightmare On Elm Street franchise.

(195) Hannibal Lector is the most famous fictional serial killer.

He is based on several killers but was also largely inspired by a sinister doctor that Thomas Harris once met.

(196) Damien: Omen II was finished by Don Taylor after the original director Mike Hodges fell out with the studio and left. Hodges directed a small chunk of the finished film we see on screen before he departed. Hodges directed some the military academy scenes and factory stuff. He also directed the opening to the film. Hodges says he worked on the film for three weeks before he was fired - or fled as the case may be. It seems no love was lost on either side but it would have been interesting to see what Hodges would have come up with if he'd stayed.

(197) Billy Campbell was the third person to play Ted Bundy. This was in the competent but routine 2003 TV film adaptation of Ann Rule's book The Stranger Beside Me. Ann Rule worked with Bundy on a suicide hotline and considered him to be a friend. The Bundy she knew was kind and considerate. You can imagine then her shock when she found out that Bundy was a serial killer - and one of the worst ones in American history to boot. Campbell is effective enough as Bundy although like Mark Harmon he's probably a trifle too Hollywood handsome for the part. Campbell's performance works because he underplays Bundy and doesn't ever resort to chewing up the scenery.

(198) Madison Wolfe, who plays the troubled little English girl Janet in The Conjuring II, is actually American in real life.

(199) John Boorman actually turned down an offer to direct the original Exorcist film - which might explain why he agreed to do the sequel.

(200) Sigourney Weaver said she talked to Ridley Scott about directing Alien 3 but he had too many films on his slate and wasn't available.

(201) Graveyard Shift is a short story by Stephen King which you'll find in his Night Shift compendium. The story is about

workers who have to combat a rat infestation in the bowels of
a factory and discover there is a rather large and pesky rodent
in their midst. There was a poorly received film adaptation in
1990.

(202) Them! is a classic 1954 black and white monster film
about giant radiated, mutated ants running amok in the New
Mexico desert and was directed by Gordon Douglas. 'A horror
horde of crawl-and-crush giants clawing out of the earth from
mile-deep catacombs!' went the blurb on the theatrical poster.
The film won an Oscar for its special effects and is regarded to
be one of the more successful examples of the sci-fi atomic age
paranoia genre.

(203) Amityville 3-D was the feature film debut of Meg Ryan.

(204) The Conjuring was called Captured by Demons in the
Czech Republic.

(205) The explosive and bombastic sequence in Predator
where Schwarzenegger and his commando team destroy a
rebel camp in the jungle was shot by second unit director Craig
Baxley. John Mctiernan, the director of the film, disliked this
sequence and tried to have it removed. Mctiernan felt that it
didn't really fit in with the tone of the rest of the movie. Baxley
had shot the sequence because he felt they needed some
spectacular footage to placate worried studio executives. It
eventually stayed in the film.

(206) The tanning booth scene in Final Destination 3 is based
on a popular urban legend.

(207) Steven Spielberg didn't like John Williams' famous Jaws
theme when he first heard it.

(208) Despite making a gazillion horror films, Peter Cushing
wasn't actually a horror fan in real life.

(209) Caroline Munro, one of the most famous Hammer

'babes', turned down a leading role in Doctor Jekyll and Sister Hyde because of the nudity in the script.

(210) Pinhead is estimated to have killed 48 people in the Hellraiser franchise.

(211) Jamie Lee Curtis turned down an offer to be in Scream 3.

(212) Donald Pleasance shot his contribution to John Carpenter's Halloween in only five days.

(213) Kwaidan is a 1964 Japanese anthology horror film directed by Masaki Kobayashi - based on stories from Lafcadio Hearn's collections of Japanese folk tales. This richly atmospheric and strikingly designed picture received an Academy Award nomination for Best Foreign Language Film. This is a very classy and artistic anthology and one of the best horror anthologies ever made.

(214) Saw is the only film series in history to have its first seven films released in consecutive years.

(215) The first Purge film only took nineteen days to shoot.

(216) Vincent Price's daughter said that he loved to take her trick or treating at Halloween.

(217) The 'knife trick' scene that Bishop does in Aliens might have been influenced by a similar scene in the 1981 slasher film My Bloody Valentine.

(218) David Cronenberg turned down an offer to direct Alien Resurrection.

(219) Oliver Hirschbiegel was supposed to direct the third Blade film but became unavailable due to his contract to make Downfall. Downfall is famously the source of many comical Hitler rant YouTube memes.

(220) Lee Van Cleef and Jerry Ohrbach were considered for the part of Gary played by Donald Moffat in John Carpenter's The Thing.

(221) Playboy cover star Marli Renfro was a body double for some the shower scene moments in Psycho.

(222) Michael Myers has killed over 150 people in the Halloween franchise.

(223) Peter Cushing was absent from an Amicus anthology for the first time in Vault of Horror as he was busy filming And Now the Screaming Starts! - also an Amicus film.

(224) Ruby Wax has a small role as the US Ambassador's secretary at the start of Omen III: The Final Conflict. Wax is an American who is well known in Britain as a television presenter, author, and comedian.

(225) Natasha Henstridge replaced Courtney Love in John Carpenter's Ghosts of Mars after Love injured her foot.

(226) The budget for 1968's Night of the Living Dead was $114,000.

(227) Blair's chilling computer analysis in John Carpenter's The Thing reads as follows: PROBABILITY THAT ONE OR MORE TEAM MEMBERS MAY BE INFECTED WITH INTRUDER ORGANISM
-75%- PROJECTION: IF INTRUDER ORGANISM REACHES CIVILIZED AREAS... ENTIRE WORLD POPULATION INFECTED 27,000 HOURS FROM FIRST CONTACT.

(228) The Texas Chainsaw Massacre 2 is a critique of eighties consumerism. Note how Drayton Sawyer is now a stressed (and not very ethical) businessman.

(229) The cultish 1981 summer camp slasher film The Burning was the feature film debut of Jason (George in Seinfeld)

Alexander, Fisher Stevens, and Holly Hunter.

(230) 2017's IT (an adaption of Stephen King's novel) is the most commercially successful horror film of all time.

(231) Gunnar Hansen had a rubber hammer to depict Leatherface hitting victims in The Texas Chainsaw Massacre.

(232) Anthony Hopkins tried not to blink as Hannibal Lecter to make the character stranger and scarier.

(233) Jack Nicholson spent three days filming the axe scene in The Shining and had to destroy 60 doors before Stanley Kubrick was satisfied.

(234) Roger's slide between the mall escalators in George Romero's Dawn of the Dead was improvised by the actor Scott H. Reiniger.

(235) Laurence Fishburne, Denzel Washington, and LL Cool J were considered for the lead role in Blade before Wesley Snipes.

(236) C. Thomas Howell said he was genuinely afraid of Rutger Hauer making The Hitcher because Hauer was so intense.

(237) Halloween III: Season of the Witch (1982) is the third instalment in the Halloween film series. It was directed by Tommy Lee Wallace. John Carpenter and Debra Hill, the creators of Halloween, returned as producers. It was decided after Halloween II to turn the franchise into an anthology with different stories and characters set around Halloween. So no Michael Myers. The film wasn't a tremendous success but is now something of a cult classic.

(238) Jessica Harper, the star of the Italian horror film Suspiria, said it was a strange experience to make the film because the dialogue was not recorded and the actors were

speaking in different languages. The film was going to be dubbed afterwards so none of this mattered.

(239) Eli Roth's Cabin fever was the most profitable horror film released in 2003. It cost $1.5 million to make and grossed well over $20 million.

(240) Jet Li was offered the part of villain Deacon Frost in the first Blade movie.

(241) 28 Days Later is a 2002 horror film directed by Danny Boyle and written by Alex Garland. The film is a British riff on George A Romero's 'Dead' series of zombie films and also borrows rather liberally from John Wyndham's Day of the Triffids novel.

(242) Jennifer Love Hewitt and Sarah Michelle Gellar were originally going to play each others roles in I Know What You Did Last Summer but they swapped before shooting began.

(243) John Carpenter shot some extra gore scenes for The Fog because he didn't think the original cut was very scary.

(244) Shaun of the Dead took nine weeks to shoot.

(245) Fans of the Predator series were excited when it was announced that Shane Black had signed to direct The Predator - the fourth film in the franchise. Black played Hawkins in the original Predator and was now an established film director. The film was co-written with Fred Dekker (of The Monster Squad fame). Production on 'The Predator' began in 2016. The film ran into trouble though when Shane Black decided the first cut wasn't scary because of all the daylight scenes. There were further problems when Olivia Munn, one of the stars of the film, was furious when she found out that Black's friend Steven Wilder Striegel had a scene in the film. Steven Wilder Striegel had been a registered felony sex offender since 2010, when he pleaded guilty to "enticing a minor by computer" after he attempted to lure a 14-year-old girl into a sexual

relationship via email. He spent five months in jail.

Munn's complaints led to executives cutting Striegel's scene from the film. Munn said she found it "both surprising and unsettling that Shane Black, our director, did not share this information to the cast, crew, or Fox Studios prior to, during, or after production. However, I am relieved that when Fox finally did receive the information, the studio took appropriate action by deleting the scene featuring Wilder prior to release of the film." Black had to offer an apology for casting Steven Wilder Striegel in the film. The release date of The Predator was pushed back but - sadly - the reshoots were all to no avail. The film was an awful mess and scored just 32% on Rotten Tomatoes. The box-office was disappointing too. Out of the (at the time of writing) four Predator films (which don't include the two Alien v Predator pictures), Shane Black had easily made the worst one.

(246) The original version of Shane Black's The Predator had two 'friendly' Predators teaming up with the human characters to fight the giant super Predator. Edward James Olmos also had a role as an army general. All this stuff was thrown on the cutting room floor in favour of the underwhelming third act we see in the actual movie. Shane Black said he would be happy for us to see the original version of The Predator but it probably won't happen because the studio are unlikely to shell out the money required to finish the special effects.

(247) Eerie Tales (Unheimliche Geschichten) is a 1919 German horror anthology directed by Richard Oswald and was perhaps the first example of the omnibus horror film. Eerie Tales is sometimes assumed to be a lost film but - happily - this is not the case. There are five stories in the film including Poe's The Black Cat, Dr Tarr And Professor Feather and Robert Louis Stevenson's The Suicide Club. The wraparound features a strange book shop where three paintings loom large on the wall. A prostitute, Death, and the Devil. When the shop closes the characters leave their paintings to enter the real world and read spine chilling stories from some of the dusty old books on

offer...

(248) The 1980 slasher film Prom Night was called Coronation of Revenge in Finland.

(249) Predators director Nimrod Antal didn't want a woman in the film but was persuaded to cast Alice Braga. They toyed with the idea of making Alice Braga's character an alien but this idea was jettisoned.

(250) Planet of the Apes star Kim Hunter had to sleep with vaseline on her face during production because the glue in her ape mask was burning her skin and giving her a rash.

(251) The cultish 1982 slasher film The Slumber Party Massacre was written as more of a spoof and satire but become a more straightish film in the end. The producer Roger Corman also made sure to add plenty of nudity.

(252) The 2009 film The Collector was originally conceived as prequel to Saw.

(253) Danny Boyle was the original director of Alien Resurrection but he bailed out after he realised that he knew nothing about special effects and would be well out of comfort zone trying to direct this film.

(254) 1990's Predator 2 famously featured a xenomorph skull in the Predator's trophy room.

(255) Lance Henriksen was offered the role of Frank in Hellraiser but turned it down. He later appeared in one of the sequels.

(256) Michael Biehn was apparently going to play a soldier at the end of Aliens vs Predator: Requiem but Fox blocked this piece of stunt casting.

(257) Jeroen Krabbé was considered for the role of Damien

Thorn in Omen III. Krabbé later played a Bond villain in The Living Daylights.

(258) Jaws: The Revenge had a preposterously tight production schedule that had the actors working seven days a week. It was edited in just six weeks to meet its release date.

(259) When he was making Aliens, James Cameron fired the original director of photography Dick Bush because Cameron felt he was making the alien nest sequences look too bright. Cameron had wanted these scenes to be darker and more eerie.

(260) A Christmas Horror Story is a 2015 anthology horror film directed by Grant Harvey, Steven Hoban, and Brett Sullivan. This is a surprisingly decent effort and better than you probably expect it to be. The framing device is not bad either. It features William Shatner as a drunken DJ named Hoban doing a radio shift over Christmas. Holban keeps reporting on some sort of trouble going on down at the mall and warns his listeners to stay away from that place. The mall is later used for a nice twist at the end of the film when we finally see what this trouble was all about. Shatner's DJ pops up several times during the film as we weave in and out of the stories.

(261) V/H/S is a 'found footage' horror anthology. There are five segments from different directors. This spawned two sequels and is sometimes cited as a film that helped to reactivate the anthology genre but I think we probably have to give Trick 'r Treat more credit for that (as retrospective as the success of that film was). Anthology horror films never really go away but finding ones that are really good is another matter entirely.

(262) I, Monster was directed by Stephen Weeks and written by Milton Subotsky. It is based on The Strange Case of Dr Jekyll and Mr Hyde by Robert Louis Stevenson. The names Jekyll and Hyde are changed in the film. Christopher Lee plays

Dr Charles Marlowe, a psychologist who becomes the wicked Edward Blake when he takes his new experimental serum. I suppose 'Dr Marlowe and Mr Blake' obviously wasn't a catchy enough title! Peter Cushing lends support as Marlowe's lawyer and friend Frederick Utterson. It is Utterson who suspects that all is not well with Dr Marlowe. This was a rather troubled production and shot in 3-D on the insistence of Milton Subotsky. The 3-D effect work was rendered useless though because the sets had been built the wrong way round.

(263) Cabin Fever 2: Spring Fever is one of those sequels that seems to be forgotten these days. Ti West, now a fairly acclaimed director, directed this film but said that the studio recut it and added new scenes - all without his participation. He asked to have his name taken off the film but apparently the 'Alan Smithee' (an official pseudonym used by film directors who wish to disown a project) option is no longer available.

(264) The grisly television studio death scene in Omen III: The Final Conflict took two weeks to film.

(265) Despite writing the film, Joss Whedon absolutely loathed Alien Resurrection. "They executed it in such a ghastly fashion they rendered it unwatchable," said Whedon.

(266) The original Friday the 13th was made on a budget of $550,000.

(267) The 2018 version of Halloween had the biggest box-office opening in the history of the franchise.

(268) One of the producers on the film Dog Soldiers lobbied for a title change to Night of the Werewolves but the director Neil Marshall fought against this.

(269) John Carpenter's first cut of The Fog was only eighty minutes long. No wonder he felt the need to shoot some extra scenes!

(270) 1965's Dr Who and the Daleks was directed by Gordon Flemyng and written by Milton Subotsky (it is said though that David Whitaker really wrote the film on the instruction of Terry Nation - Nation allowing Subotsky to have the screen credit as along as Whitaker was brought in as a writer). The film is loosely based on the 1963 television episodes The Dead Planet. This was the first of two films Amicus made based on the famous BBC television show. Amicus bought an option from Terry Nation and the BBC to make two Dr Who films for the modest sum of £500. I bet you couldn't do that today! Dr Who and the Daleks is a film that consciously separates itself from the television source so much that it is not considered to be part of the Doctor Who canon or history. In this film, the Doctor is not an alien Time Lord from the planet Gallifrey but an eccentric human inventor. William Hartnell was not asked to reprise his television role as the Doctor for this film and so the Doctor is instead played by Amicus favourite Peter Cushing. This version of the Doctor is a bumbling sweet grandfather who is smart but sort of clumsy. The Doctor in the story is a professor and inventor on Earth who has invented an incredible machine called the TARDIS which can travel through space and time.

(271) Many of the zombie extras in Shaun of the Dead were Spaced fans (Spaced is a TV show that Edgar Wright, Simon Pegg, and Nick Frost were involved in) recruited through the Spaced website.

(272) 2006's V for Vendetta was directed by James McTeigue and written by The Wachowski Brothers. It is based on Alan Moore's classic comic. After the disappointing movie adaptations of The League of Extraordinary Gentlemen and From Hell, a disenchanted Moore wanted nothing to do with this film and asked for his name to be taken off the credits. He later complained that the film altered his key concept of fascism v anarchism.

(273) Horror audiences are remarkably diverse demographically. There is no one specific type of horror fan.

(274) The Canadian actor William Hope read for the part of Hudson in Aliens but played Gorman in the end.

(275) Patrick Swayze was going to make a cameo in Zombieland but he sadly passed away before this could happen.

(276) The director's cut version of Alien is 117 minutes. Oddly, even though Ridley Scott added a couple of new scenes, it's actually a minute shorter than the standard 116 minute theatrical cut.

(277) Stalker is a 1979 Soviet science fiction film directed by Andrei Tarkovsky. The premise of the film is a dangerous expedition launched to investigate to a mysterious restricted area called the Zone. The decayed and dust laden look of the 'Zone' in Stalker was an important influence on the design of the Upside Down in the TV show Stranger Things.

(278) The makers of the 1987 film Hellraiser were very annoyed when the famous British film critic Barry Norman (who had a weekly film review show on the BBC) trashed the movie. They were especially irritated because it was for all and intents and purposes a British film industry movie and they felt as if Norman should be more supportive. As a consequence of this they invited Norman to visit the set of Hellraiser II. During his visit Barry Norman confessed to them that he just didn't like horror movies - which would explain why he'd hated Hellraiser. Norman conceded to them though that films should be judged on their individual merit - regardless of what genre they fell into.

(279) John Carpenter was heavily courted to direct Exorcist III but in the end decided to pass on this offer.

(280) James Wan, director of the first Saw movie, said the situations were often based on some nightmares he had as a child.

(281) Reese Witherspoon declined the part of Sid in Wes Craven's Scream.

(282) Kurtwood Smith was cast against type as the villain in Robocop. The director Paul Verhoven gave Smith rimless glasses to make him look like Heinrich Himmler.

(283) Mercedes McCambridge supplied the demonic voice of Regan in The Exorcist.

(284) Evan Rachel Wood turned down the part played by Emma Stone in Zombieland.

(285) On the set of Hellraiser, Clive Barker instructed Doug Bradley to be very minimal in his movements because Pinhead was not the type of person who needed to do anything to be threatening.

(286) 1985's Creature (aka Titan Find) is a science fiction horror film directed by William Malone. What we have here is another entry in the subgenre of Alien clones. The premise has a corporation (Alien and its clones certainly got it right when they predicted a future where huge corporations were more powerful than governments) encountering a strange alien laboratory on the moon of Titan. Creature is never quite as much fun as you want it to be. The early scenes of the idiots in the strange alien lab lead you to anticipate a much more satisfying B-movie experience. However once this early plot activation device is done the pacing is a little on the slow side.

(287) The character of Dr Wren was in Alien Resurrection was written with Bill Murray in mind but Murray - wisely perhaps - was clearly not interested.

(288) 2014's As Above, So Below is a found footage horror film set in the tunnels and catacombs underneath Paris. As Above, So Below is sort of like a horror version of Tomb Raider with the treasures and objects leading to great danger and supernatural terror. The catacombs make for an intriguing

setting and if you are claustrophobic like me then watching people crawl through narrow gaps is terrifying enough without ghosts or monsters. As Above, So Below is not The Descent but it passes the time and is nowhere near as bad as its reviews would suggest.

(289) Mel Gibson turned down the part of Seth Brundle in the remake of The Fly.

(290) 2005's Constantine was directed by Francis Lawrence with a screenplay by Kevin Brodbin and Frank Cappello, the film is based on Vertigo Comics' Hellblazer comic book, with plot elements taken from the "Dangerous Habits" story arc (issues #41–46) and the "Original Sins" story arc. John Constantine was created by Alan Moore and Stephen R. Bissette, and first appeared as a supporting character in The Saga of the Swamp Thing #37 (June 1985). As a suicide survivor, demon hunter John Constantine (Keanu Reeves) has literally been to hell and back -- and he knows that when he dies, he's going to Satan's realm unless he can earn enough goodwill to climb God's stairway to heaven. While helping policewoman Angela Dodson (Rachel Weisz) investigate her identical twin's apparent suicide, Constantine becomes caught up in a supernatural plot involving both demonic and angelic forces. Constantine was not a huge financial success and met with a mixed critical reception. Time seems to have been relatively kind to the film now and it's picked up a modest cult following over the years. The main difference between the comics and the film is that the streetwise British magician is now an American gumshoe who deals with the occult. It's best just to regard this film as it's own thing as the name of the character aside it's not too faithful to the comics.

(291) John Malkovich also turned down the part of Seth Brundle in Cronenberg's remake of The Fly.

(292) The sequel to Saw was greenlit on the weekend the first film opened.

(293) Roy Scheider is said to have signed up to the helicopter action film Blue Thunder just to make sure he was busy and unavailable for Jaws 3. "Mephistopheles couldn't talk me into doing it," he said of Jaws 3. "They knew better than to even ask."

(294) Ricco Ross initially turned down the part of Private Frost Aliens to appear in Kubrick's Full Metal Jacket. James Cameron persuaded him to leave Kubrick's film and take a part in Aliens instead.

(295) 1985's Night Train to Terror is an anthology directed by Jay Schlossberg-Cohen, with segments directed by John Carr, Phillip Marshak, Tom McGowan, and Gregg C. Tallas. Like some other bargain basement horror compendiums this was patched together from different films. The films in question are Cataclysm, Death Wish Club and Scream Your Head Off. These films exist in various forms though Scream Your Head Off was never actually completed. Night Train to Terror is an eccentric attempt to wring some money from these doomed projects.

(296) There has been a huge increase in the amount of horror movies produced in the last decade. Explanations for this include the fact that technology has made it easier to film and distribute movies. Even if you don't have much money up your sleeve you can still make a low-budget horror film.

(297) According to a study, 42% of horror fans are female.

(298) 7'2 Nigerian visual artist Bolaji Badejo was inside the xenomorph suit in Alien. Badejo was a student in London at the time and spotted by agent Peter Archer in a pub. Archer knew that Alien required a very tall and thin actor to wear the xenomorph suit.

(299) The creature costumes worn by Bolaji Badejo in Alien cost $250,000 to produce.

(300) When New line dubbed American accents into the British set Hellraiser to make it seem like it was set in America, they even planned at one point to have an actor dub over Doug Bradley as Pinhead. Thankfully, good sense prevailed in the end and Bradley's performance was left intact.

(301) John Landis was one of the background apes in Battle for the Planet of the Apes and later claimed that special effects maestro John Chambers, who designed the ape costumes in Planet of the Apes, was responsible for the alleged Bigfoot film famously shot by Roger Patterson at Bluff Creek. Chambers later debunked this myth and said he'd had nothing to do with any Bigfoot hoax.

(302) Oliver Reed turned down the part of Quint in Jaws when it was offered to him by Richard Zanuck.

(303) John Carpenter was supposed to direct Zombieland but at the time it was merely the pilot for a proposed television show. When it became a full-fledged movie Carpenter dropped out because he didn't want to commit himself to such a lengthy project.

(304) Eli Roth said he got the idea for Hostel from stories about the 'dark web' (where it is claimed you can do all sorts of alarming things - like arrange for someone to be killed).

(305) The Texas Chainsaw Massacre features a real skeleton in one of the scenes.

(306) Linda Blair was never really able to turn her role in The Exorcist into a credible acting career. After a couple of fairly well recieved television movies she slid into more television movies, low-budget horror, and comedies. She also seemed to be frequently cast in trashy 'women in prison' movies. She was never really in a big movie again after The Exorcist II - although the 1980 film Roller Boogie was quite popular in its day. Blair wasn't the most talented or natural actress and so once she aged out of 'cute teenager' roles her career was more

or less over.

(307) Alien was actually toned down for release to make it less gruesome. Parker was originally supposed to die in a more blood drenched way and have his head crushed by the Alien. Brett was supposed to have his heart removed by the xenomorph - the crew finding him with a hole in his chest.

(308) Silent Night, Deadly Night Part 2 is a 1987 horror sequel to 1984's Silent Night, Deadly Night. The first film featured a maniac who goes on a killing spree dressed as Santa Claus. It became highly controversial (which seems hard to believe these days) and gained a certain noteriety as a result. This 1987 sequel revolves around Ricky (Eric Freeman), the brother of the maniac from the first film. Ricky goes on his own killing spree and more carnage ensues. This sequel was directed by an editor named Harry Lee. Apparently, he was asked to simply cut and mix the footage from the first film to create the illusion of a sequel but he insisted on being allowed to shoot something new. Nonetheless, an awful lot of footage from the first film is shown to us again so if you have seen the original Silent Night, Deadly Night you might well feel a bit cheated.

Silent Night, Deadly Night Part 2 is one of those films that is so bad it has become something of a cultish comedy staple on YouTube. Much of this is thanks to the atrocious acting of Eric Freeman as our murderous main character. Freeman's line readings are very amusing at times. The actual film (what there is of it away from the flashbacks) is rather cheesy and silly compared to the first film. Silent Night, Deadly Night was not Ingmar Bergman but it did feel more competent and atmospheric than this sequel. Silent Night, Deadly Night Part 2 is good for a laugh but that's about it really.

(309) The Riverman is a 2004 television film based on Robert Keppel's 2004 non-fiction book The Riverman: Ted Bundy and I Hunt For the Green River Killer. It was written by Tom Towler and directed by Bill Eagles. Bruce Greenwood plays Keppel and Cary Elwes plays Ted Bundy. Gary Ridgway (the

'Green River' serial killer that Keppel is hunting) doesn't really feature much in the film and is played by Dave Brown. The story is more about how Keppel became intrigued by Bundy and how being in close proximity to such an evil man affected him. The focus of the film is on Keppel and The Riverman is absorbing enough as TV movies go. Bundy doesn't feature much - which is sort of refreshing because we don't have to trawl through the (already too familiar by now) Ted Bundy story yet again. We merely meet Bundy in prison a few times in this TV movie. The Capture of the Green River Killer was a 2008 TV movie (again) about the Gary Ridgway case. James Marsters played Ted Bundy and John Pielmeier played Gary Ridgway. The Capture of the Green River Killer has some decent reviews although I'm not quite sure why we needed two television movies about the same subject. The Riverman was perfectly competent and would have sufficed on its own.

(310) Live and Let Die is the only James Bond film to have overt horror influences.

(311) George Romero's Day of the Dead was shot in the Wampum mine, a former limestone mine near Pittsburgh, that was being used for an underground storage facility.

(312) Rob Zombie helmed a remake of Halloween in 2007. John Carpenter was critical of this film for having too much backstory about Michael and thus (in Carpenter's view) destroying some of the mystique about the character.

(313) The Wicker Man was called The Cursed Scarecrow in Greece.

(314) Shelley Long auditioned for the part of Veronica in The Fly. At the time she was about to leave the sitcom Cheers. David Cronenberg later seemed to imply that Long's audition was a disaster. To be fair to Shelley Long her strength was comedic roles.

(315) John Jarratt lived in the Australian outback for a time to

prepare for playing Mick Taylor in Wolf Creek.

(316) Sigourney Weaver did not get top billing in the credits for Alien because they didn't want to give the audience any clues that her character would be the sole survivor. Added to this is obviously the fact that Weaver was fairly unknown at the time.

(317) The Purge broke the record for the biggest box-office opening of an original r-rated horror movie. The Conjuring would soon break this record though.

(318) Crystal Lake in Friday the 13th was a real summer camp. It was called Camp No-Be-Bo-Sco.

(319) Jason Vorhees has killed 170 people in the Friday the 13th franchise.

(320) Zombieland was originally going to be called Another Day in Zombieland.

(321) Carrie Henn, who played "Newt" in Aliens, did not pursue an acting career and later became a teacher.

(322) The War of the Worlds is a 1953 science fiction horror film directed by Byron Haskin from a script by Barre Lyndon. The film was the first screen adaption of the classic HG Wells novel and won an Oscar for its colourful and striking special effects. This is a rather loose adaption of the story written by HG Wells with late Victorian London replaced by fifties California and the central protagonist now bespectacled square-jawed physicist Dr Clayton Forrester (Gene Barry).

(323) Abe Sapien in the Hellboy universe is a homage to Gill-Man in Creature from the Black Lagoon.

(324) Anthony Shaffer, screenwriter of The Wicker Man, felt that Edward Woodward and Britt Eklund were miscast in the film.

(325) The part of Captain Dallas in Alien was offered to Harrison Ford but he declined.

(326) Jeremy Irons turned down the part of Hannibal Lector in The Silence of the Lambs.

(327) Jeff Bridges turned down the role of MacReady in The Thing.

(328) Early posters and teasers for Alien 3 suggested the aliens were going to reach Earth. False marketing indeed!

(329) Brad Pitt, Christian Slater, and John Stamos all unsuccessfully auditioned for teen roles in A Nightmare On Elm Street.

(330) John Lithgow turned down the lead role in David Cronenberg's The Fly because he found the script a bit gross for his liking.

(331) The Uncanny is a 1977 British/Canadian horror anthology film directed by Denis Heroux. This is probably second only to Tales That Witness Madness (where Joan Collins memorably found out her husband had fallen in love with a tree) for sheer ludicrousness when it comes to seventies horror anthologies with neither film having anything to do with campy seventies horror portmanteau masters Amicus. The Uncanny offers three tales of horror all revolving around cats and opens in Montreal where nervous author Wilbur Gray (the great Peter Cushing) goes to visit his publisher Frank Richards (Ray Milland) with his latest book - all the while being secretly followed by a black moggy. Gray has written about flying saucers and the secrets of the pyramids in the past but his latest offering looks set to be his most eccentric work yet. The dubious publisher listens as Gray explains that he has discovered that cats secretly run the world and his book will prove it!

(332) Robin Williams was seriously considered for the part of

Jack Torrance in Kubrick's adaptation of The Shining.

(333) Despite her status as a legendary horror icon, Jamie Lee Curtis says she never watches horror films in real life because she finds them too scary.

(334) Courteney Cox, Tracey Gold, Jennifer Grey and Demi Moore all auditioned for the part of Nancy in A Nightmare On Elm Street.

(335) The Legend of the 7 Golden Vampires is a 1974 Hammer film directed by Roy Ward Baker. The film is a fusion of vampire horror and kung fu capers designed to take advantage of (then) current trends and was a co-production between Hammer and Hong Kong's Shaw Brothers Studios. The Legend of the 7 Golden Vampires is possibly the most eccentric film Hammer ever made and one that connoisseurs of strange cinema will probably get a kick out of.

(336) Lance Henriksen arrived in London to shoot Aliens with a selection of knives in his luggage as he wanted to master the knife trick scene for his android character Bishop. He had some explaining to do when customs officials discovered the knives.

(337) Hostel II was banned in New Zealand.

(338) Ridley Scott described Alien as a cross between Star Wars and The Texas Chainsaw Massacre.

(339) Gunnar Hansen had to wear heels as Leatherface in The Texas Chainsaw Masacre to make him taller than the rest of the cast.

(340) The first Resident Evil film was made in Germany.

(341) Aliens star Jenette Goldstein (who played Vasquez) is now the proprietor of a large-cup bra business.

(342) Bill Murray improvised the line about Garfield in Zombieland.

(343) Though set in Alaska, 30 Days of Night was shot in New Zealand.

(344) The director of Paranormal Activity shot the film in his own house.

(345) Davidson Military Academy in Omen II: Damien is really Northwestern Military and Naval Academy in Lake Geneva, Wisconsin.

(346) The bees used in the production of Candyman were very young bees. This was so their stings would be less dangerous.

(347) It Came From Outer Space was released in 1953 and directed by Jack Arnold in his first venture into science fiction/horror. It was written by Harry Essex from a screen treatment by Ray Bradbury (who based it on a story he wrote called The Comet) and emerges as a well made and enjoyable piece of fifties paranoia that plays like a cross between Invasion of the Body Snatchers (which of course was made a few years after this film) and an episode of The Outer Limits. This was the first of these types of films to really exploit the possibilities of a lonely desert location and its themes of human duplication and loss of identity would become a cliche soon enough but were obviously a lot fresher and less well worn in 1953

(348) The 2009 Japanese film Grotesque was banned in Britain. The British Board of Film Classification argued that the film, unlike other 'torture porn' movies, offered no narrative, exposition, or character development, and simply had sadistic torture for the sake of it.

(349) The controversial movie A Serbian Film was banned in Germany, Norway, Brazil, Australia, New Zealand, Malaysia, Spain, and Singapore.

(350) Some viewers are a bit confused by Evil Dead II and wonder why on earth Ash has gone back to that dreaded cabin. The truth is, it isn't really a true sequel in that this version of Ash has never been to the cabin before. The film is more of a remake than a sequel in the strictest sense.

(351) Cinemaholic.com ranked the lawnmower scene in Peter Jackson's Brain dead as the goriest scene in any horror movie. Julia's revival in Hellbound: Hellraiser II was ranked second.

(352) Believe it or not, Psycho is the first American movie to show a toilet onscreen.

(353) Dan O'Bannon said that the characters in his original Alien screenplay were gender fluid (in that they just had surnames) and that John Travolta was considered for the part of Ripley at one point.

(354) David Cronenberg cut some gore scenes (like one where Brundlefly eats a foot) from The Fly after preview audiences were grossed out.

(355) The Thing from Another World is a 1951 science fiction/horror film. Although Christian Nyby is officially listed as the director it seems to be an open secret and generally accepted that the film was in fact directed by Howard Hawks. Nyby worked as an editor on several Howard Hawks films and it appears that Hawks directed The Thing from Another World himself and then simply arranged for Nyby to get a directing credit as a favour.

(356) Sarah Michelle Gellar was in line to play Alice in the first Resident Evil film before Milla Jovovich was cast.

(357) Alien: Covenant was originally going to be called Aliens: Paradise Lost.

(358) Although set in North London, the interior scenes in The Conjuring II were shot in Los Angeles. They spent about ten

days shooting in London for exterior scenes.

(359) Only about a dozen horror movies have made over $300 million at the box-office.

(360) The insurance company on Predator insisted that actor Sonny Landham could only be hired if he was given a bodyguard. "Not to protect Sonny, but to protect other people from Sonny," said John Mctiernan. Landham, who plays the spiritual Indian soldier Billy in the film, was a famed loose cannon away from the camera.

(361) Benicio del Toro was supposed to have the lead role in The Predator but he was to busy to do it in the end.

(362) Ridley Scott's Alien was called The Eighth Passenger: Death in Hungary.

(363) Witchfinder General was called There is No Mercy for the Executioner in Serbia.

(364) The actor John Jarrett said he took months to come up with Mick Taylor's creepy laugh in Wolf Creek.

(365) Peter Cushing named 1968's The Blood Beast Terror as the worst film he'd ever been in.

(366) The early eighties film Don't Go in the Woods seems laughably amateurish today with very unconvincing gore effects but it actually ended up on the banned video nasty list in Britain.

(367) Peter Jackson turned down an offer to direct Child's Play 3.

(368) Amityville 3-D was the film debut of Meg Ryan.

(369) Danny Boyle didn't direct 28 Weeks Later (which was obviously a sequel to his film 28 Days Later) because he was

busy making Sunshine. He did direct the terrific opening sequence though.

(370) Leatherface: The Texas Chainsaw Massacre III was finally released in 1990 and flopped badly. The film had to undergo extensive cuts to gore scenes to secure a rating and this not only delayed its release but also made the film less coherent. The director Jeff Burr was amazed whe he viewed the film in the cinema because it was only then that he realised the studio had shot an entirely new ending for the movie behind his back!

(371) You may notice that Charlton Heston has a slightly raspy voice in Planet of the Apes at times. This is because he was suffering from the flu while shooting some of it.

(372) The iconic M41A1 Pulse Rifles used in the film Aliens were named and designed by James Cameron and brought to life by the British prop and armoury company Bapty & Co.

(373) Michael Caine, Anthony Hopkins, James Mason, and Terence Stamp turned down the part of Colonel Caine in Tobe Hooper's Lifeforce. In the end it was Peter Firth who played this part (and he played it very well).

(374) Peter Duffell, the director of the Amicus film The House That Dripped Blood, wanted to call the film Death and the Maiden but obviously didn't get his way in the end. According to Duffell, Peter Cushing and Christopher Lee also agreed with him that The House That Dripped Blood was a "lousy" title.

(375) Peter Yates and Jack Clayton were both approached to direct Alien but turned down the offer.

(376) Peter Jackson claims he passed on an offer to direct Alien Resurrection because the prospect didn't excite him.

(377) Corin Nemec played Ted Bundy in the 2008 film Bundy: An American Icon. This was by far the weakest of the Bundy

films because it was less a drama and more of a schlocky straight to DVD horror film. Bundy: An American Icon was pretty awful by any standards. Nemec looks far too old to be playing Ted Bundy (this is obviously even more pronounced in the college scenes) and the film features hammy acting and headache inducing flashbacks. Horror icon Kane Hodder even turns up as a judge at the trial - which probably tells you all you need to know about how serious a film Bundy: An American Icon turns out to be.

(378) A cinema usher fainted during an early screening of Alien in Britain - thus ensuring its legend.

(379) A thousand actresses were considered for the nude space vampiress part memorably played by Mathilda May in Tobe Hooper's Lifeforce. They included Marina Sirtis and Elizabeth Sladen. Mathilda May has seven minutes of screen time in the film. She was a former dancer and spoke no English.

(380) Ash's car in The Evil Dead actually belonged to Sam Raimi. The car made a cameo in many subsequent Sam Raimi films.

(381) Brooke Shields and Janeane Garofalo were up for the part of newswoman Gale Weathers in Scream.

(382) The Purge was a very low-budget movie which couldn't afford to pay the actors much money. Despite this Ethan Hawke agreed to be in the film because he was a friend of the producer and director.

(383) All the characters in Cube are named after prisons.

(384) Noah Schnapp was up for the part of Richie Tozier in Stephen King's IT before Finn Wolfhard was cast. Schnapp and Wolfhard were both cast in Stranger Things soon after.

(385) Amanda Bearse couldn't return for the Fright Night sequel because she was contracted to the (dark and cultish)

sitcom Married... with Children.

(386) During the production of the famously troubled David Fincher film Alien 3, Empire magazine visited the set and were privvy to some candid observations from cast members. "We're having a grand old time on this one. I haven't got a bloody clue what's happening," said Brian Glover, who was playing the warden Andrews. "I've done about 50 films and TV dramas and they're paying me more on this than the rest put together. Good job they have, too, 'cause I don't think it will ever be finished. Sigourney's a down-to-earth woman but the director keeps on changing the bloody script after I've learned the lines!"

(387) Apparently the Weinsteins nearly fired Wes Craven from Scream because they didn't think it was very scary. They were won over in the end though when they saw more footage.

(388) The script for Hellbound: Hellraiser II had to be considerably altered when the actor Andrew Robinson declined to return for the sequel.

(389) Although he is often remembered as the star of The Silence of the Lambs, Anthony Hopkins was only in the film for about nineteen minutes.

(390) Saw III only took 27 days to shoot.

(391) Hellraiser: Bloodline has some scenes which take place on a space station in the future. This 'space' section was supposed to make up a third of the film but many of these scenes were cut after studio meddling.

(392) George Romero wanted to put footage from his previous zombie films in the credits of Land of the Dead but he couldn't get the rights.

(393) The crop circles you see in the M. Night Shyamalan film Signs were done for real and not CGI.

(394) One of the reasons why Geena Davis was cast in The Fly is because she was very tall and therefore wouldn't look too small next to Jeff Goldblum.

(395) One of the actors in the raft segment in Creepshow 2 ended up with hypothermia. He was able to come back and finish his scenes after hospital treatment.

(396) Robert Carlyle was offered the role of Major Henry West in 28 Days Later. Carlyle would later take a role in the sequel.

(397) Predator 2 was going to be set in New York but the studio decided it would be cheaper to have the film take place in Los Angeles.

(398) The role of the 'Creeper' in Jeepers Creepers was originally written with Lance Henriksen in mind.

(399) Heather Donahue, the female lead in The Blair Witch Project, later retired from acting and changed her name to Rei Hance. She said that using her real name in Blair Witch was a mistake and it stopped her from getting acting work.

(400) The film company who made the folk horror classic The Wicker Man called it the worst film they had ever seen when it was screened for them.

(401) Donald Pleasance was considered for the part of Blair in The Thing.

(402) The original distributor of The Texas Chainsaw Massacre was the Bryanston Distribution Company - which turned out to be a Mafia front operated by Louis Peraino.

(403) The actor Nicholas Ball said some cast members walked off set of Tobe Hooper's Lifeforce at one point because Cannon had run out of money and some people hadn't been paid.

(404) Dick Richards was going to direct Jaws before Steven

Spielberg came onboard. Richards directed films like The Culpepper Cattle Company and Farewell, My Lovely.

(405) Sarah Michelle Gellar was going to play Sasha Williams in Urban Legend but had to drop out due to her commitments on the TV show Buffy the Vampire Slayer.

(406) Reese Witherspoon and Melissa Joan Hart both claimed to have turned down roles in I Know What You Did Last Summer.

(407) Alex was going to be in the second Final Destination film but negotiations fell through with actor Devon Sawa.

(408) Renny Harlin was originally hired to direct Alien 3 but was frustrated by the confused and drawn out development of the film and left the production. Harlin wanted the story to be about finding the planet where the aliens come from but the producers told him this would be too expensive and said that the story should take place on a space station. Harlin though this was a boring idea and so departed.

(409) The creatures in Gremlins were animatronic puppets that cost between $50,000 and $65,000 apiece.

(410) John Carpenter didn't want to direct Halloween II but he did agree to write it though to make some money as he felt he'd been shafted on the profits from the first film.

Carpenter chose a young director named Rick Rosenthal to helm Halloween II and completed his script. When Carpenter saw a preview of the finished film, he felt it wasn't very scary and seemed tame when compared to the bubbling stew of slasher films abounding. So he organised three days of reshoots and added more gore and nudity into the story.

Rosenthal was said to be annoyed at Carpenter's changes and felt they ruined the pacing of Halloween II. He'd wanted the film to be more suggestive than explicit.

(411) Lector's 'okey dokey' catchphrase in Hannibal was made up by Anthony Hopkins.

(412) Leatherface was not allowed to utter a coherent line in The Texas Chainsaw because they didn't want the character to convey any intelligence.

(413) The helicopter pilot at the end of Predator is Kevin Peter Hall - who also plays the Predator.

(414) Juliette Binoche and Robin Wright were offered the role of Ellie Sattler in Jurassic Park.

(415) Though we think of Cannon as a somewhat bargain basement studio, Tobe Hooper had a bigger budget on Lifeforce than he did on Poltergeist with Steven Spielberg.

(416) Damien Thorn in Omen III was the first major role for Sam Neil. Neil later said he didn't think much of the film or his own performance.

(417) Adrien Brody was an Oscar winning actor and unlikely casting as the lead in Predators because he'd never done action roles. Director Robert Rodriguez said Brody was perfect casting though because real life soldiers look lean and plausible (as opposed to muscle bound hulks like Arnold Schwarzenegger).

(418) Contrary to some assumptions, Anthony Perkins enjoyed playing Norman Bates and did feel like it was a millstone around his neck.

(419) Dan O'Bannon wrote the role of Frank for himself in Return of the Living Dead but thought James Karen was so good that he should have the part instead.

(420) Mickey Rourke, Michael Keaton and Kenneth Branagh were all considered for the role of Jack Crawford in The Silence of the Lambs.

(421) Caroline Williams ran into her Texas Chainsaw Massacre 2 audition screaming to make an impression on Tobe Hooper.

(422) Diane Cilento (ex-Mrs Sean Connery) was persuaded out of semi-retirement for the part of the island's school teacher, Miss Rose, in The Wicker Man.

(423) Stephen King hated the film version of his story Children of the Corn so much that he vowed never to have anything to do with any future films or sequels relating to this story.

(424) James Woods is yet another actor who turned down the part of Seth Brundle in the remake of The Fly. It seems that most actors in Hollywood gave this film a very wide berth.

(425) Millicent Simmonds, who plays the deaf young daughter in A Quiet Place, is deaf in real life.

(426) The giant monster who turns up at the end of the 2020 deep sea horror thriller Underwater is Lovecraft's Cthulhu.

(427) Joe Dante was in contention to direct a 1980s remake of Creature from the Black Lagoon but Universal got cold feet and scrapped the project after Jaws 3 bombed.

(428) The Amicus producers said it was always easier to hire Peter Cushing than Christopher Lee because Cushing would accept less money than Lee.

(429) The cultish monster film Tremors was called In the Land of the Rocket Worms in Germany.

(430) 1970's Mumsy, Nanny, Sonny and Girly (aka 'Girly') was directed by Freddie Francis and written by Brian Compton. The film is based on a stage play by Maisie Mosco entitled Happy Family. Although this film is rather obscure, Francis considered it to be his best work as a director. This is a bizarre horror black comedy and quite possibly a brilliant one too. The film takes place at a grand sprawling country mansion where a

family have retreated in a strange fantasy world apparently based on children's books. The family are Mumsy (Ursula Howells), Nanny (Pat Heywood), and the children Sonny (Howard Trevor) and Girly (Vanessa Howard). Although Sonny and Girly wear school uniforms and are treated like children they look rather on the mature side for such treatment. The family play something they call the 'Game'. This involves luring men back to the house - the men then indoctrinated into the rules of the house and forced to behave like children too. If they don't obey the rules they are 'sent to the angels' - in other words they are killed. Whenever a 'friend' is killed, Sonny records it and they watch the murder on a projector.

This is the sort of film that is better watched then described. It's a strange film but a very compelling one. The tension arises when a man played by Michael Bryant arrives at the house after Sonny and Girly kill his companion (played by Imogen Hassel) in a park by grabbing her foot when she is on top of a slide in a playground. Bryant goes with them to the house to lay low and is blackmailed because they have the body of the woman in the house. However, Bryant's character observes the family and their bizarre game and concludes that the key to his survival is to get close to Girly. This will create a fracture in the family as Girly won't want to 'share' her new friend - especially when he awakens her sexuality. This is a beautiful looking film (shot at Oakley Court) and amusingly bizarre and deadpan. There are some great performances in the film but the star is unquestionably Vanessa Howard as Girly. Vanessa Howard is fantastically arch and charismatic and gives a brilliant performance. The tragedy of this film's failure to find an audience was that Howard abandoned acting soon afterwards. A terrific shame. The only casting complaint you might have is that the rather plain looking Michael Bryant doesn't really seem like the sort of person who would charm and excite Vanessa Howard but then his performance is very good. Mumsy, Nanny, Sonny and Girly is a jet black comedy full of memorable scenes and deadpan wit.

(431) During the filming of Jurassic Park the film's central shooting location – the Hawaiian island of Kauai – was hit by Hurricane Iniki.

(432) Josh Brolin, Matt Damon, James Marsden, Jason Priestley, Keanu Reeves and Mark Wahlberg were all in contention to play the lead character Rico in Starship Troopers.

(433) The Vincent Price film Theatre of Blood was called To Kill or Not to Kill, That is the Question in Spain.

(434) Linda Blair declined the chance to be considered for the lead role in the Brian De Palma film adaptation of Stephen King's Carrie because she feared becoming typecast as innocent vulnerable victims in horror movies. Carrie White is a troubled girl who has to deal with both the scorn of her peers at school and her overbearing Bible crazed mother. However, Carrie has powerful telekinetic abilities and can only be pushed so far.

(435) The 1963 film The Haunting is considered to be a classic today but - strangely - it was not much of a hit when it was first released.

(436) The Howling was called Scream of Horror in Brazil.

(437) Arnold Schwarzenegger was supposed to have a cameo at the end of Predators but this never happened in the end.

(438) Harry Dean Stanton said he took the role of the police detective in John Carpenter's Christine because it was rare for him to be offered such a 'normal' sort of part.

(439) If you've ever wanted to see an Esperanto language horror film starring William Shatner then you are in luck. Incubus, written and directed by Leslie Stevens in 1966, is exactly that. Stevens brought in his Outer Limits team of Dominic Frontiere and Conrad Hall to work on the film but it

was all to no avail. The film bombed and was even said to have been cursed. The evidence for the curse? One of the actors killed himself, Leslie Stevens got divorced and saw his business empire ruined, and most prints of the film were destroyed in a fire.

Another spooky element of the alleged curse is that Sharon Tate and Roman Polanski attended the premiere. For thirty years Incubus was thought to be a lost film until a print was discovered in a Paris basement (for some reason France was the only country that seemed to like the film when it first came out). It was said that Esperanto speakers were angered by the film because the actors (who had to learn their lines quickly) spoke a gibberish version of Esperanto that made no sense. William Shatner said he experienced first hand evidence of this Esperanto speaker backlash while he was making Star Trek and someone threw a rock through his dressing room window! It all sounds like a joke but apparently it really happened.

The film itself is set in a small village and concerns a young soldier named Marc (Shatner) who becomes tangled up with a young succubus named Kia (Allyson Ames). Kia is supposed to shephard sinners to hell but wants to find a pure soul to lead into the darkness. That would presumably be much more of a challenge. She targets Marc but love complicates matters. Despite the obscurity of this picture and its general reputation as that 'crazy Esperanto William Shatner film', Incubus is actually better than you expect it to be. This is like some surreal experimental lost episode of The Outer Limits that has suddenly come to light. The decision to use Esperanto works in a way because (as was the intention) it gives the film an appropriately weird 'nowhere' sense of time and place. Who the hell knows where or when this is supposed to be taking place? That's the point. The film is quite stylish too and has a wonderfully surreal atmosphere. This is not a lost masterpiece but it's by no means bad for a film that was shot in just two weeks. The film feels inspired by the (then cultish) works of the reclusive Swedish director Ingmar Bergman and plays like an attempt to make an art house B-horror movie. There are some very atmospheric sequences shot at a ranch and on the beach. The story is somewhat incoherent at times (probably best not to expect airtight logic in this sort of film!) but it's an experience and Shatner is actually very good. If you are fond of eccentric B-movies and have a weakness for black and white horror movies then Incubus is probably worth a look.

(440) Orion wanted Arnold Schwarzenegger to play Alex Murphy/Robocop but Schwarzenegger wasn't interested. Armand Assante tested to play Alex Murphy/Robocop. Michael Ironside was cast at one point but eventually made way for Peter Weller.

(441) The mechanical shark built for Jaws at great cost rarely worked. Steven Spielberg took to calling the mechanical shark the Great White Turd.

(442) The director Stephen Hopkins said he wanted to cast John Lithgow as Keyes in Predator 2 but the studio insisted on Gary Busey.

(443) Kirsten Dunst was originally cast as Ivy Walker in the M. Night Shyamalan film The Village but dropped out to do another movie.

(444) Richard Dreyfuss, Pierce Brosnan, and William Hurt were all courted for the lead role of Seth in The Fly remake before Jeff Goldblum was cast. Many actors turned this part down because they didn't want to have to go through the extensive make-up prosthetics required.

(445) Bill Murray was the first choice to play the lead in the film version of The Dead Zone but Christopher Walken played the part in the end.

(446) The working title for the George Romero film The Crazies was The Mad people.

(447) The original idea for the sequel 28 Weeks Later was that an SAS team would have to go into a zombie infected London to rescue the Prime Minister.

(448) Stephen Hopkins, the director of Predator 2, said he had to resist studio pressure trying to persuade him to cast Steven Seagal as Mike Harrigan.

(449) It was something of a miracle that such a memorable monster emerged in Predator because the film started shooting with a completely different alien design. Martial arts star Jean Claude Van Damme (then largely unknown) had been hired to play the Predator (the thinking was that his athleticism would make the alien appear quick and formidable) and the alien costume he was given looked like a cross between a fly, a prawn and a dog with a big yellow eye and spindly legs like stilts. It was atrocious and after shooting a couple of sequences (where it looked like a risible monster from SPACE 1999) John McTiernan sent the Predator costume back to the studio and told them the film would be a laughing stock if he carried on like this.

When production was shut down, Arnold Schwarzenegger stepped in and asked special effects expert Stan Winston (with whom he had become friends while making The Terminator) if he could come up with anything to save the picture. Winston was inspired by illustrations of Rasterfarian warriors he'd seen and came up with a new Predator that had dreadlocks and a steel mask and looked much more like a fearsome warrior hunter than the other design. The diminutive Van Damme (who had done nothing but complain about the heat anyway) was sacked and they hired the 7 foot plus Kevin Peter Hall to play the Predator instead. Schwarzenegger now looked puny next to the Predator. That was the point.

(450) Tom Savini wanted to play Captain Rhodes in Day of the Dead but George Romero didn't agree to this. Romero presumably wanted Savini to focus on the zombie make-up and gore effects.

(451) Cillian Murphy initially tried to do an English accent in 28 Days Later but it sounded too fake so they just let him speak in his real Irish accent.

(452) The enjoyable Hammer film Captain Kronos: Vampire Hunter (which is a sort of horror swashbuckler) had its release delayed for two years (it was made in 1972 but only saw the light of day in 1974) and was given zero marketing. No wonder it bombed - which is a shame.

(453) Rob Zombie didn't want to make a sequel to his 2007 version of Halloween and only agreed to do so in return for financial backing for Lords of Salem.

(454) The Return of the Texas Chainsaw Massacre is the fourth film in the franchise and first screened in 1994. It was later retitled Texas Chainsaw Massacre: The Next Generation and given a wider release in an attempt to cash in on the fact that its two leads - Renee Zelwegger and Matthew McConaughey- had both become big Hollywood stars.

(455) William Hurt was the first choice to play the twin gynecologists in David Cronenberg's Dead Ringers. Hurt wanted to do the film but was unavailable due to existing commitments.

(456) Linda Hamilton turned down the female lead role in the remake of The Fly because she found the script too gross and disturbing.

(457) Michael Cera unsuccessfully auditioned for the part of the little boy in The Sixth Sense.

(458) Tobe Hooper's film The Funhouse was caught up in the 'video nasty' panic and banned in Britain for a time. This seems unfair as the film is fairly tame by horror standards and a good movie.

(459) The 1981 film The Burning was only passed uncut by the

British Board of Film Classification in 2002. It was doubtless the raft scene and the early scissors murder that made the censors so jumpy.

(460) It was Steven Spielberg who arranged for Jan de Bont to direct the 1999 remake of The Haunting for Dreamworks. Spielberg had actually developed this project with Stephen King at one point. Legend has it that Spielberg stipulated that his name be taken off all the promotional material when he saw how bad the film was.

(461) The main reason Joshua Leonard got a plum role in The Blair Witch Project is that he knew how to use a camera.

(462) The 2000 film adaptation of the Bret Easton Ellis novel American Psycho featuring Christian Bale as the consumerist serial killer Patrick Bateman was not a big financial blockbuster but it was cultish enough to get a sequel - of sorts - a few years later. American Psycho 2 (aka American Psycho II: All American Girl) began life as just a generic thriller with no connection to the original but the American Psycho 2 name was tagged onto it almost as an afterthought. So it became a (straight to DVD) sequel to American Psycho. This move irritated not only Bret Easton Ellis but also Mila Kunis - the star of American Psycho 2. "When I did the second one, I didn't know it would be American Psycho 2. It was supposed to be a different project, and it was re-edited, but, ooh ... I don't know. Bad." Kunis plays a woman named Rachael who studies criminology and starts bumping off academic rivals to win a coveted teaching assistant position. The criminology professor who she manipulates is played by William Shatner. It's hard to take Shatner very seriously given his facility for self-parody over the years but to be fair to him this isn't the most serious of films to begin with.

The film rather clumsily tries to connect the two films by revealing that Patrick Bateman once attacked a young woman who was looking after the Kunis character when she was a child. Kunis stabbed Bateman with an icepick and so - in a symbolic sense - picked up his baton, or dagger perhaps. Unsurprisingly, Christian Bale had nothing to do with this rather contrived late in the day sequel and so Batmeman is played by another actor and only seen in flashbacks. American Psycho 2 plays like a very forgettable made for television thriller and doesn't have much DNA in common with the original film. Kunis is no Christian Bale and the supporting cast is rather bland. There are plenty of twists but no real surprises as the murder spree of Rachael spins out of control when she plots her way to the teaching position. Even if you did like the first you are probably best off ignoring this very loose and not very memorable sequel.

(463) Emma Stone auditioned for the part of Laurie Strode in the 2007 Halloween remake.

(464) Wes Craven was vocal about hating the Freddy vs. Jason film.

(465) Bryan Singer and Paul WS Anderson were candidates to direct Alien Resurrection.

(466) Creepshow III has nothing to do with George Romero or Stephen King. Somehow or other, a company called Taurus Entertainment got the rights to the Creepshow name and inflicted this abomination on us.

(467) Inseminoid is a 1981 sci-fi horror film directed by the cultish Norman J Warren. This is often dubbed an Alien copycat although the makers insist it was written before Alien came out. Whatever the truth there are some obvious similarities. The key difference is that Alien is an expensive and well made film while Inseminoid was shot in four weeks in some caves in Kent. There is a Roger Corman quality to Inseminoid and the film it sort of resembles is Corman's cheapjack Galaxy of Terror. But Galaxy of Terror had a young James Cameron working on the designs and special effects and is well made for a film of its type. Inseminoid is jarringly amateurish and bargain basement and doesn't make an awful

lot of sense. It has a little notoriety though, mainly thanks to an alien rape scene involving the wholesome Judy Geeson.

(468) The French director (Jean-Pierre Jeunet) of Alien Resurrection spoke no English and had three translators on the set.

(469) Alien vs Predator is said to have ruined a chance of James Cameron and Ridley Scott returning to make a new Alien film together.

(470) The interesting 1998 found footage horror film The Last Broadcast was shot on video for just $900.

(471) Land of the Dead, for some reason or other, was banned in Ukraine.

(472) The Birds II: Land's End is a 1994 television film sequel to the Hitchcock classic directed by Rick Rosenthal. There is no good reason for this film to exist and after watching it you can only wish it didn't. I'm sure the cast do. Brad Johnson and Chelsea Field are a grieving couple who move to a small island town with their young daughters. The local birds start acting strange and attacking people etc. The bird attacks are ok when they arrive but - unfortunately - the rest of the film is deadly dull with a glacial pace and bland performances. Hitchcock's style and playful humour is sorely missed - as is Rod Taylor. Tippi Hedren turns up for a small part but apparently regretted it and later called the film embarrassing. Hedren doesn't even play the same character that she played in the original film. Rick Rosenthal obviously agreed with everyone that Birds II was a bad film and decided to go down the Alan Smithee route when it came to this clunker. He wanted his name off the film. The Birds II: Land's End is a very forgettable television film that shamelessly tries to trade on a famous movie name to draw attention.

(473) 1977's The Incredible Melting Man is something of a cult film today although only because it is a famously bad one. The

film was written and directed by William Sachs. The plot has astronauts encountering a deadly burst of radiation while on a space mission to Saturn. Colonel Steve West (Alex Rebar) is the only survivor but on his return to Earth he wakes up in a hospital to discover that something most alarming has happened as a consequence of the radiation. West seems to be slowly melting! He's soon on the run and completely insane, murdering whoever he runs into.

Here's the strange thing about The Incredible Melting Man. Sachs wrote and directed the film as a spoof of old sci-fi horror films. It was supposed to be a comedy. However, the producers Max felt that a 'straight' horror film would be more lucrative so they basically changed the film from a comic one into a horror film and inserted several new hastily filmed scenes - all of this done without Sachs (who later predictably complained that his original intent had been ruined). So, as a consequence, The Incredible Melting Man is a bizarre mix of the silly and the horrific. You have Rick Baker's enjoyably disgusting melting man effects and several 'horror' moments like a head floating in a river but you also get lashings of Ed Wood style ineptitude and some of the worst acting you've ever seen in your life. The Incredible Melting Man is though, for better or for worse, an experience if nothing else.

(474) Hellraiser: Bloodline was the last Hellraiser film to get a theatrical release.

(475) Tony Todd claims he was once approached about a Candyman v Leprechaun movie (which would obviously have been in the vein of Freddy vs. Jason). Todd said he wanted nothing to do with what he thought was a silly idea.

(476) Sam Raimi wanted the third Evil Dead film to be called The Medieval Dead. It obviously ended up as Army of Darkness.

(477) Shaun of the Dead's release was pushed back a few weeks to avoid a clash with Zack Snyder's Dawn of the Dead.

They evidently felt that audiences wouldn't be in the mood to watch TWO zombie films on the same weekend.

(478) James Cameron made the cast of Aliens undergo real military training in preparation for the shoot. Sigourney Weaver, William Hope, and Paul Reiser were excluded from the military exercises because their characters were 'outsiders' in the film.

(479) The ghostly mist engulfed town of Silent Hill in the video game and movie series were big influences on the look of the Upside Down dimension in Stranger Things.

(480) The Fly II, the sequel to David Cronenberg's 1986 remake of The Fly failed to replicate the success of the original. This 1989 sequel was directed by Chris Walas and doesn't have Jeff Goldblum (for understandable reasons as he turned into a giant fly and died in the first film!) or Geena Davis. The Davis character makes a brief appearance but is played and voiced by another actress. This sequel revolves around the son of Goldblum and Davis. Martin Brundle (played by Eric Stoltz) lives in the Bartok Industry labs (they were the company who funded the teleporting device in the first film). He's more or less a prisoner and they are eager to learn about his abilities and the science of his father's work. Martin is growing at a rapid rate for his age and has great intelligence.

You wouldn't say this sequel is a flat out terrible film because it has a competent cast and direction but it is a very unpleasant and unnecessary one. If you can watch the mutant dog scenes you are clearly possessed of a stronger stomach than me. It is at this point that the film loses a lot of viewers I suspect - and rightly so. There should be a special place reserved in hell for scripts that put animals in peril or horrible situations purely for dramatic effect. Eric Stoltz is a decent actor but the story here is never that interesting and he can't hold the screen in the same way that Jeff Goldblum did. It's hardly original also to have a sinister company meddling in science they don't understand and keeping a human science experiment under lock and key. Daphne Zuniga, a competent actress, is required to play a rather stupid character as the love interest and when Martin goes all 'MartinFly' and the special effects kick in you'll probably know all too well where we are heading and that bad stuff is on the way for corporate villain Bartok. The Fly II is decently made but completely unnecessary all the same.

(481) Bloodbath at the House of Death is a 1983 horror spoof. This was a vehicle for the comedian (and radio presenter) Kenny Everett. Bloodbath at the House of Death was forgotten relatively quickly but it does seem to induce fond memories in those who liked Everett and recall it coming out at the time. This film is no lost masterpiece and like many horror spoofs struggles to stretch the joke out to a feature length running duration but one could argue that it rather anticipates films like Scary Movie and Shaun of the Dead with its mixture of horror and comedy.

Bloodbath at the House of Death is certainly no Shaun of the Dead but it's not as bad as its casual reputation would suggest. In the film Kenny is Dr Lukas Manderville, the head of a team of scientists who investigate Headstone Manor, a reputedly haunted residence where dark things once happened. Needless to say there are soon spooky shenanigans aplenty as blood sloshes around and people are bumped off. Bloodbath at the House of Death is watchable but very wise to adopt a skimpy 88 minute running time. There is only so far to take this type of horror pastiche before boredom sets in. Everett is pretty good in a rare film role and Pamela Stephenson lends solid support as his nerdy assistant Dr Barbara Coyle. Stephenson was a prolific fixture around this time in films and tv as she was attractive and could be funny. There are a lot of familiar faces in the film. Don Warrington of Rising Damp, Gareth Hunt of The New Avengers, Cleo Rocos (from Kenny's television show), Graham Stark from the Pink Panther films, and horror icon Vincent Price. Price does his thing in cult robes and although I'm sure he had no idea what he was even acting in here his glorified cameo makes the film much more cultish than it might have been. You wouldn't be missing out

on the greatest experience ever known to man if you skipped
Bloodbath at the House of Death but it's certainly not as bad as
its reputation would have it.

(482) The film version of The Dead Zone stars Christopher
Walken as a man who can see people's future just by shaking
hands with them. It is one of the better Stephen King
adaptations.

(483) The 1975 movie Death Race 2000 takes place in a
dystopian future which has a violent car race where you get
points for running over pedestrians.

(484) A scene in Alien where the alien creature corners
Lambert and does a strange 'crab walk' over to her was deleted
from the finished film. It doesn't quite work but it is
undeniably creepy.

(485) The classic 1974 horror film Black Christmas was called
A Blood-Red Christmas in Italy.

(486) The entertaining home invasion horror film You're Next
sat on the shelf for two years because of studio trouble. A
shame as it deserved a wider audience.

(487) Halloween franchise star Danielle Harris played a
teenager in 2007's Halloween remake despite being in her
thirties at the time.

(488) Brazil is a 1984 inspired dystopian black comedy. Terry
Gilliam actually had to shame the studio into releasing Brazil
because they couldn't make head nor tail of it.

(489) Blood Bath is a 1976 bargain budget horror anthology
directed by Joel M Reed. Reed is best known for the gruesome
exploitation film Blood Sucking Freaks. Despite its title, Blood
Bath is a much tamer affair and actually has a PG rating. You
might not go into this film expecting much but it's not bad for
what it is. The stories would slot fairly well into something like

Tales from the Darkside and the cast are better than you expect from a film that clearly has a non existent budget and an amateurish sort of feel (in terms of production). You can tell that the cast are in the joke here. They know this film is supposed to be tongue-in-cheek and they amusingly pitch their performances accordingly. The framing device is simple and effective enough. A horror film producer named Peter Brown (Harve Presnell) has dinner with some guests and says that - despite his profession - he doesn't believe in the occult. They all then share some stories aimed at perhaps dissuading him from his point of view.

(490) Silent Hill was called The Curse of the Valley in Portugal.

(491) Al Adamson was a writer/producer/director of exploitation films in the 1960s and 1970s. He was responsible for cultish obscurities like Psycho A Go-Go (later worked into Blood of Ghastly Horror), Satan's Sadists, Horror of the Blood Monsters, Dracula Vs. Frankenstein, and Five Bloody Graves. These grade Z drive-in pictures featured biker chicks, gore, and general low budget mayhem and fun for those with a sweet tooth for tongue-in-cheek schlock. The decline of the drive-in market affected Adamson's stock-in-trade and by the 1990s he was more or less retired and in his sixties.

Vulnerable from the recent death of his wife (and frequent leading lady) Regina Carro, he became friendly with 50-year-old builder Fred Fulford. Fulford became a live in contractor helping out with renovations at the house. Fulford would be responsible for Adamson's macabre death, the director meeting a fate akin to a character in one of his films. In 1995, Adamson was reported missing by his brother and friends when they didn't see him for weeks. The chief suspect was Fulford. When Adamson was found dead and buried in cement where a Jacuzzi had been, Fulford was tried and convicted of the murder. Deputy District Attorney Paul Vinegrad maintained, based on pathology results, that Fulford had bashed in Adamson's skull with a heavy object, then dumped his body in the pit and poured four tons of cement over the crime scene. "This really is an overwhelming case of guilt," Vinegrad said. It didn't quite end there. It transpired that Fulford had taken to wearing Adamson's clothes and used his credit cards to pay for items. Adamson, a kind and well liked character by all accounts, had clearly made an error of judgment when he became friends with Fulford. Perhaps Fulford, clearly a disturbed and dangerous individual, hid his darkness well. The end result was tragic.

(492) Nick Nolte, Ed Harris, Peter Coyote, and Scott Glenn all turned down the role of MacReady in The Thing.

(493) Lost Boys: The Tribe is a 2008 straight to DVD sequel to the cult 1987 film The Lost Boys. This film was directed by PJ Pesce. Eighties kids will have fond memories of The Lost Boys and should probably avoid Lost Boys: The Tribe, which, even by the standards of straight to DVD films, is very poor indeed. The premise of the film is a rehash of the original and has a pair of teenagers becoming mixed up with a group of vampire surfers when they move to a small town in California.

Corey Feldman returns as vampire hunter Edgar Frog and (as usual) overacts in horrendous fashion. The rest of the cast is a no name affair aside perhaps from a cameo by Tom Savini at the start. The now sadly departed Corey Haim is absent apart from a scene at the end. The vampires in the film are deadly dull and just annoying. A far cry from the original film, where the vampires were led by a charismatic young Kiefer Sutherland. Lost Boys: The Tribe is a terrible film trading on the name of the first film to sell some DVDs. This will be a severe disappointment to anyone curious enough to give it a whirl. A third (straight to DVD) Lost Boys film appeared later and was rather forgettable too. It's probably best for everyone to just enjoy the first film and pretend that these sequels don't exist.

(494) In 1986, the De Laurentiis company produced a sequel to their King Kong remake titled King Kong Lives with John

Guillermin back in the director's chair. The premise of the sequel is that Kong didn't die at the end of the first film. He is given a heart transplant and revived. He is also given a mate in the form of Lady Kong - a giant female ape. The pair are soon on the run in the United States with the military in hot pursuit. This film was an absolute turkey in 1986, bombing at the box-office and earning Razzie nominations. The only consolation for the producers was that it was a rather low-budget affair compared to the original. Linda Hamilton, only a few years after her breakthrough in The Terminator, seems rather embarrassed to be here as one of the main leads and John Ashton is the predictable army villain. King Kong Lives is a terrible film by any standard but - in mitigation - it is mildly entertaining merely by being so bonkers. If you can't glean at least a small degree of pleasure from King Kong and his ape girlfriend invading a golf course then there is probably no hope for you.

(495) I Know What You Did Last Summer was one of the more successful (in financial terms) of the modern teen slashers that abounded in the wake of Wes Craven's Scream. The sequel, I Still Know What You Did Last Summer, was quick out of the blocks and directed by Danny Cannon. The film has Jennifer Love Hewitt and friends on a trip to a tropical island where - once again - they find themselves being stalked by a vengeful bogeyman. The first film was no classic but it did make money and was competent on most levels. This sequel never really justifies its own existence and feels like pretty thin gruel as far as these retro nineties slashers go. Wes Craven's Scream series struggled to maintain its own high standards through three sequels so it certainly isn't easy to keep repeating this sort of formula without it appearing as if the well has run dry. I Still Know What You Did Last Summer, despite only being the second film (there was later a straight to DVD third film) in the series, already seems to show there isn't really anywhere you can take this premise. We didn't really need to see Jennifer Love Hewitt being stalked by a deranged fisherman again. The film made some money but the reviews were brutal. The current Rotten Tomatoes tally for I Still Know What You

Did Last Summer is a miserable 7%.

(496) The 'werewolf break' (where the viewer is invited to guess which character the werewolf is) in the camp but fun Amicus film The Beast Must Die was added in against the wishes of the director Paul Annett.

(497) Two of the Colonial Marine actors in Aliens, Tip Tipping (Private Crowe) and Trevor Steedman (Private Wierzbowski) - both sadly no longer with us - were British stuntmen. Tipping had also served in the SAS - a famous special forces unit of the British Army. Tipping died in a 1993 parachuting accident.

(498) Jonathan Demme and Jodie Foster declined to return for Hannibal (the sequel to The Silence of the Lambs) because they found Thomas Harris' novel distasteful.

(499) The biggest complaint people had about Prometheus is the stupidity of the characters. Trying to pet a vicious looking alien snake, getting lost in caves despite mapping them on a computer, trying to outrun a falling spaceship when it would be easier to just move to the side. What's going on with Sean Harris as the stupid thuggish geologist Fifield? Here he is on the scientific jaunt of a lifetime and he acts like a schoolboy who's been forced to go to school on a rainy Monday morning.

(500) Ellen Page (now Eliott Page) was supposed to play the lead role in Sam Raimi's Drag Me to Hell. An actor's strike nixed this though and Page became too busy thereafter - thus paving the way for Alison Lohman to play the part.

(501) Joe Dante declined an offer to direct Halloween III.

(502) Aliens vs Predator: Requiem, like its predecessor, was not screened for critics. This is a standard firefighting tactic by studios when they know they have a clunker on their hands and want to avoid a rush of advance negative reviews.

(503) An early plan for Jason X was to have the film set at

Crystal Lake in winter snow. In the end though we got Jason in space.

(504) The Abominable Dr. Phibes was called The Bloodthirsty Avenger in Sweden.

(505) The cult classic Horror Express was called Zombie Express Bound to Hell in Japan.

(506) Peter Cushing was supposed to be in The Abominable Dr. Phibes but he dropped out when his wife fell ill. He was replaced by Joseph Cotten.

(507) Wes Craven's The Hills Have Eyes was originally going to be called Blood Relations: The Sun Wars.

(508) Tobe Hooper didn't allow the cast of the Texas Chainsaw Massacre to visit the locations until they started shooting. The heat and grisly nature of the Sawyer house therefore came as unpleasant shocks.

(509) Stephen King famously disliked Kubrick's adaptation of The Shining. King later wrote a TV film adaptation which he felt was more faithful to his book.

(510) Hereditary was called The Legacy of the Devil in Latin America.

(511) Betsy Palmer has top billing in Friday the 13th but only really appears near the end.

(512) Saw III was intended to be the last film in the franchise but the studio asked for the ending to be changed so that more sequels would be possible.

(513) During the production of Silence of the Lambs, Anthony Hopkins deliberately provoked Jodie Foster off-camera by mocking her West Virginia accent. He did this to create an edge to their scenes together.

(514) John Cusack was considered for the role of Arnie Cunningham in Christine.

(515) The big sequence in Predator 2 where the special forces military team try to catch the Predator in the frosty slaughterhouse was a nightmare to shoot and took four weeks to complete.

(516) Halloween: Resurrection is the eighth instalment in the Halloween film series. It was directed by Rick Rosenthal, who had also directed Halloween II in 1981. This is a terrible film after the fairly enjoyable H20 and was widely panned by fans of the franchise. An internet reality show is being organised by businessman Freddie (Busta Rhymes) and will broadcast from the old Myers home. A bunch of students will be equipped with cameras and spend a night there in a Ghostwatch/Most Haunted type of affair. However, Michael gatecrashes the event and starts killing everyone. Halloween: Resurrection's premise is too gimmicky and - even worse - this surveillance footage/internet reality type of thing was old hat even by 2002.

(517) Hellbound: Hellraiser II was banned in the Australian state of Queensland for quite a while.

(518) 1983's Screamtime is a curious horror anthology with a slightly mysterious existence. Three short British films by Michael Armstrong and Stanley A Long are turned into a compendium with a bizarre new framing sequence in New York that someone cobbled together as a wraparound. Screamtime is a strange film it has to be said. A bit grubby and homemade but genuinely creepy at times.

(519) Kim Hunter was cast as Zira in Planet of the Apes after Julie Harris and Shirley Maclaine decided it wasn't for them. Hunter said she spent so much time looking at Roddy McDowall made up to look like a chimpanzee she forgot what he looked like in real life. Planet of the Apes lead actor Charlton Heston bumped into Kim Hunter without her

monkey make-up after shooting wrapped and had no idea who she was!

(520) Aliens was a somewhat fractious production as the British crew at Pinewood didn't care for the blunt no nonsense workaholic style of James Cameron. The British crew had never heard of James Cameron and had no guage of his talents because they hadn't seen The Terminator yet. At one point there was friction when Cameron complained about the crew's union scheduled breaks to have a cup of tea!

(521) The interior of the bleak Yorkshire pub The Slaughtered Lamb in An American Werewolf in London was filmed back in London and the pub's clientele consists mostly of local stage actors. Rik Mayall was invited to be in the film (Mayall is one of the characters in the Slaughtered Lamb) after John Landis saw him perform at a comedy club.

(522) Linda Blair was in the midst of drug problems at the time Exorcist II: The Heretic was made. She was rarely on set at the right time. Blair said Richard Burton was often drunk near the end of the production but quite charming all the same. Burton said he only did the film to pay for his divorce. This sequel got famously bad reviews. William Friedkin, who made the original, called it the worst film he'd ever seen. William Peter Blatty, who wrote the first film, said the audience were openly laughing at Exorcist II: The Heretic during a preview screening he attended.

(523) Sigourney Weaver did not want to do Alien Resurrection but eventually agreed when they offered her eleven million dollars.

(524) Night Skies was a sci-fi horror film Steven Spielberg planned to make to the early eighties about a family in an old farmhouse who battle aliens intent on dissecting them for research purposes. A sort of cross between Close Encounters and Gremlins. John Sayles wrote a script and Rick Baker spent months on the aliens and FX - only to be horrified (and deeply

annoyed) when Spielberg told him one day he was making a 'nice' alien film instead, that film of course being E.T.

(525) It took three days to shoot the scene in The Shining where the blood gushes from the elevator.

(526) A portion of the dialogue in The Descent had to be dubbed in later during ADR. This is because the cave sets were fake and therefore when the actors talked it didn't sound like they were in a real cave.

(527) Vincent Price's daughter said that out of the horror films he made he liked Theatre of Blood the most.

(528) 1995's Village of the Damned is a remake of the 1960 British film. A so-so later John Carpenter film, Village of the Damned is far below his very best work of the seventies and eighties. Carpenter said he was never really into this film much and only did it as part of a contractual obligation.

(529) 1986's Psycho III was directed by Anthony Perkins. This third Psycho film was poorly received and didn't make any money, sending the franchise to television for the fourth entry (which in turn didn't seem to follow the continuity of the movie sequels). This one feels very 1980s with a more avant-garde music score and more blood and gore. It's more like a generic serial killer film than the others. Anthony Perkins is still very good as Norman - although the film doesn't feel as tightly constructed as the second film and seems to lose its way a few times. It has a penchant for the bizarre too with the strange opening (a homage to Vertigo) and a weird scene where Jeff Fahey seduces a woman using light bulbs.

(530) The original title for Child's Play was Batteries Not Included. They had to alter this plan when they learned that Steven Spielberg was actually producing a film with that same title.

(531) Malcolm McDowell and Roddy McDowall were

considered for the role of Pennywise in the 1990 IT miniseries.

(532) The gas station in The Texas Chainsaw Massacre later became a bed and breakfast.

(533) Saw II took only 25 days to shoot.

(534) James Remar was the original Hicks in Aliens but let go a few weeks into shooting because of a drug problem at the time. Documentaries about Aliens (understandably perhaps) gloss over this but Remar admitted in an interview many years later that he messed up and it damaged his relationship with Walter Hill (who was a producer on the series) for many years. At the time the story was that Remar and director James Cameron had parted ways over creative differences but this was merely a smokescreen. In some of the alien hive sequences in Aliens where Hicks has his back to us, it's actually still Remar and not Biehn in the film. This is because complex scenes had already been shot before Biehn arrived and would be too expensive and time consuming to reshoot.

(535) Danny Boyle, Robert Rodriguez, George Romero, and Sam Raimi all turned down a chance to direct Scream before Wes Craven was chosen.

(536) Director Michael Wadleigh was removed from the 1981 werewolf film Wolfen in post production. Wadleigh's cut of the movie was four hours long!

(537) The director John McTiernan lost 25 pounds shooting Predator in Mexico because he refused to eat the local food.

(538) The aerial photography in The Wicker Man was partly done in South Africa because Scotland in October had bare trees.

(539) Jaws was a very difficult production because there were so many other boats in the area that Spielberg frequently had to wait for hours to get the shots of empty waters he needed

for when the three main characters are out hunting the great white shark in isolation. Because of delays and problems with the mechanical shark and the weather, Spielberg shot all of the dry land scenes first simply for something to do.

(540) An early script for Alien Resurrection had no Ripley and featured Newt from Aliens being resurrected as a clone.

(541) In the film Hannibal, Lecter seems to have a fondness for eating human brain. In reality it would highly dangerous to eat human brains. Infected prions mostly inhabit the brain.

(542) Bill Paxton, Danny Glover and Adam Baldwin from Predator 2 were sought to appear in Aliens v Predator: Requiem but nothing came of this.

(543) 1988's Scarecrows was written and directed by William Wesley. This film was fairly obscure for a while but seems to have become modestly cultish in retrospect. Scarecrows is about five bank robbing mercenaries and war criminals who steal three million dollars from Camp Pendleton and take two hostages, a pilot and his daughter. However their best laid plans threaten to be scuppered when one of them steals the money and parachutes out. The criminals land the plan and set out to find him. It's a dark night though and they find themselves in murky fields dotted with scarecrows. They will eventually discover that these scarecrows are not exactly harmless. If you can get past the so-so acting (this is a distinctly no name cast) then Scarecrows is quite a nifty little horror that makes the most of its isolated setting and - naturally - makes the most of the spooky scarecrows too. It turns out that these scarecrows are haunted demonic scarecrows (or something) and they start bumping off the criminals. Some of the deaths are very nasty. This is a film with bite.

(544) Michael York was in line to play Damien Thorn in Omen III: The Final Conflict but in the end was unavailable due to other commitments.

(545) John Carpenter's In the Mouth of Madness was called The Lair of Madness in France.

(546) Jamie Lee Curtis only agreed to appear in Halloween: Resurrection on the condition that her character Laurie Strode be killed off.

(547) 10 Cloverfield Lane was directed by Dan Trachtenberg. Michelle (Mary Elizabeth Winstead) is a young woman leaving her boyfriend. She packs up and drives off but is involved in a car crash. She wakes up in a stark dingy underground room and seems to be the prisoner of Howard (John Goodman) - a big and somewhat intimidating man. Michelle thinks that Howard must be crazy and has kidnapped her. It turns out that she's in a bunker that Howard built. He's some sort of conspiracy/survivor obsessive and used to be in the armed forces. He claims that a catastrophe created havoc above and they must stay in the bunker. A young man named Emmett (John Gallagher Jr) is also down there and seems to back up Howard's stance. Michelle adjusts to life in the bunker but she starts to become ever more suspicious of Howard, his past, and his motives. Is the world above ruined or is he lying to them?

The film's biggest problem though is that it didn't seem to know what to do as the ending. They go for a very far out twist that is ludicrously staged and feels way too derivative of a gazillion other films. I was waiting for a killer Rod Serling style ironic twist but we never actually got one. 10 Cloverfield Lane is a good tense thriller with some fine performances. It doesn't quite go the distance but is still well worth watching.

(548) Anthony Hickox's Waxwork was released in 1988. This is a wildly inconsistent and rather eccentric film but it is worth watching if you have a weakness for eighties horror. The strangest thing about Waxwork is the shifting tone. Sometimes it's a cheesy comedy, sometimes a wooden teen film, at other times a gorefest. Waxwork even has a few interludes where it seems to be taking itself seriously.

(549) Anthony Perkins initially turned down Psycho II and so the producers planned for Christopher Walken to play Norman Bates in the sequel. In the end though Perkins agreed to do the film when he read the script.

(550) Kevin Bacon was offered the role of Arnie Cunningham in Christine but chose to make Footloose instead.

(551) Re-Animator was called The Malevolent Serum in Portugal.

(552) The 1979 film The Driller Killer became a notorious banned 'video nasty' in Britain thanks mainly to its lurid cover picture of a man being drilled in the head. The actual film is not nearly as violent.

(553) The cult 2000 werewolf film Ginger Snaps was banned from some British cinemas over claims that it promoted teen violence.

(554) Wes Craven cast Neve Campbell in Scream after watching her in the TV show Party of Five.

(555) Thinner was directed by Tom Holland and written by Michael McDowell and Holland. It is based on the novel by Stephen King (as 'Richard Bachman'). The premise? Billy Halleck (Robert John Burke) is a wealthy and grossly overweight small town lawyer who seems to live a fairly charmed life. One night though, while driving, his wife (Lucinda Jenney) 'distracts' him and he runs over and kills an old gypsy woman named Suzanne Lempke (Irma St. Paule). Billy uses his powerful connections and friendships in the town to essentially quash the case against him. Judge Cary Rossington (John Horton) and Police Chief Duncan Hopley (Daniel von Bargen) cover up the details and the case is dismissed as an accident. However, the deceased woman's elderly father Tadzu Lempke (a scenery chewing Michael Constantine) curses Billy as he leaves court and whispers the word "thinner". Billy soon starts to lose weight. He's pleasantly

surprised at first but quickly realises something is wrong. No matter how much he eats he keeps becoming thinner and thinner.

Robert Burke lost twenty pounds to play the emaciated Billy in the later scenes. Originally they were going to have loose flesh hanging off Billy as he lost weight but they decided this was too horrific.

(556) The spaceship in the original Planet of the Apes film was designed by Academy Award winning Art Director William Creber.

(557) Stacey Nelkin, who played Elle in Halloween III, was briefly Woody Allen's girlfriend in the 1970s and the inspiration for Mariel Hemingway's character in Manhattan.

(558) The working title for Galaxy of Terror was Mindwarp: An Infinity of Terror.

(559) Heather Langenkamp said she had nightmares about Freddy Krueger while shooting A Nightmare on Elm Street.

(560) In the original plan for Texas Chainsaw Massacre 2, Stretch was going to be Lefty Enright's illegitimate daughter.

(561) The London Underground station used in the film An American Werewolf in London is Tottenham Court Road. (562) An early plan for the lamentable horror sequel Aliens vs Predator: Requiem had the Predator taking on a special forces team in Afghanistan but 20th Century Fox vetoed this idea as they felt it might be too expensive for the budget they had in mind.

(563) The names of the characters in Dan O'Bannon's original Alien script were Standard, Roby, Broussard, Melkonis, Hunter, and Faust.

(564) Yul Brynner got shot in the eye with wadding from a

blank cartridge during one scene in Westworld and his cornea was scratched.

(565) Shaun of the Dead was called L'alba dei morti dementi (Dawn of the Demented Dead) in Italy.

(566) Vincent Price was an art collector, a gourmet chef, and an expert gardener with an incredible cymbidium orchid collection.

(567) In his memoir Adventures in the Screen Trade, the writer William Goldman aims some barbs at The Stepford Wives - which seems to be a film that he has no real time for (I quite like it myself). He saves a lot of his sarcasm for the director Bryan Forbes casting his unknown British wife in the film at the last minute. "If you're going to kill your wife and bring her back as a robot, you wouldn't choose Nanette Newman."

(568) Guillermo del Toro says his dream project is to adapt Lovecraft's At the Mountains of Madness. At the Mountains of Madness is one of Lovecraft's most famous and enduring stories and remains hugely influential. The story is set in the lonely windswept interior of the Antarctic plateau and told by Professor William Dyer - a geologist from Miskatonic University. Dyer's terrible tale is a warning to a planned scientific expedition of Antarctica not to travel to this frozen outpost and follow in his footsteps. He led a team of scholars from Miskatonic University there to extract geological and biological specimens but what they found was so horrifying that his official report had to be censored. Ancient pre-human alien life forms, a lost city, biological engineers who dissect humans for experimentation, creatures so indescribably hideous that one look at them would lead to insanity, and giant, er, penguins. Generally, Lovecraft's pantheon of Elder Things and his rather bleak take on the universe. A vast random indifferent place without any spiritual meaning where man is inconsequential. Dyer and his team have barely hit the ice when their dogs start to act strangely and bark all the time.

Strange blob creatures millions of years old are found in a cave and this will merely be the tip of the (ahem) iceberg. "I could not help feeling that they were evil things - mountains of madness whose farther slopes looked out over some accursed ultimate abyss..."

(569) Chocolate syrup was used for blood in George Romero's Night of the Living Dead.

(570) The film World War Z is based on a 2006 book by Max Brooks - the author of 'The Zombie Survival Guide'. The book is yet another riff on George A Romero's classic 'dead' series of films and presents a scenario where the zombie epidemic was a worldwide phenomenon, leading to a protracted battle for control of the planet between the living and walking dead. In World War Z the war has been won and the crisis is now almost under control. We learn about the history of the epidemic and the war through a selection of prominent eyewitnesses in different countries who survived it - the book coming in a series of 'interviews' rather than chapters with the interviewer's questions in bold. From a crew member of a stolen Chinese nuclear submarine to someone who was holed up in Windsor Castle with the Queen, the story of how the world coped with an inexplicable zombie epidemic is told.

(571) Siskel & Ebert both complained about the 3-D in Amityville 3-D. They said it was 'crummy' and made their eyes hurt.

(572) Brad Pitt auditioned for the role of Mike in Phantasm II.

(573) Charlie Sheen auditioned for the role of Charlie Brewster in Fright Night but he was deemed to be too good looking. They wanted more of a 'boy next door' type so cast William Ragsdale instead.

(574) The Return of the Living Dead was called Zombies Are Not Vegetarians in Greece.

(575) Sam Raimi asked Edgar Wright to direct Drag Me to Hell but Wright couldn't do it because he was too busy making Hot Fuzz.

(576) Freddy Krueger's glove can be seen on the wall in a scene in Evil Dead II.

(577) The Amityville Horror was called For God's Sake, Get Out! in Finland.

(578) There were plans to make a sequel to 1981's My Bloody Valentine set in an amusement park but this obviously never happened in the end.

(579) Although the Neil Marshall film Doomsday takes place mostly in Scotland it was largely shot in South Africa.

(580) The Danish title for The Descent is Descent Into Hell

(581) The Burning was going to have a sequel set in some underground caves but it never got made in the end.

(582) John Backderf, who knew the future serial killer and cannibal Jeffrey Dahmer at school, wrote a comic called My Friend Dahmer - which was later turned into a film. My Friend Dahmer is certainly a well made and interesting film that is worth watching. Backderf said there was always a darkness about Dahmer and he wasn't the sort of person you'd want to be alone with. Believe it or not, Marvel star Jeremy Renner played Jeffrey Dahmer is a 2002 film simply called Dahmer.

(583) Madhouse was directed by Jim Clark and written by Ken Levison and Greg Morrison. It was based on the book Devilday by Angus Hall. This was a co-production between Amicus and American International Pictures. You get AIP legend Vincent Price heading up the cast and he's joined by Amicus and Hammer legend Peter Cushing. As if that wasn't enough, you also get Count Yorga himself Robert Quarry. Madhouse is not perfect but it is a lot of fun and the pairing of Price and

Cushing makes it one not to miss for any Amicus or horror fan.

(584) The 'Blob' in the 1958 film was made from red dye and silicone.

(585) Stephen Geoffreys, who played Evil Ed in Fright Night and appeared in Hollywood productions like Heaven Help Us, The Twilight Zone, and Amazing Stories, later became a performer in gay porn films. By any standards that was a pretty bizarre career change.

(586) Kyra Schon played the little girl who turns into a zombie in Night of the Living Dead. Schon said that when she is supposed to be eating her father in the film she was really eating a sandwich with some chocolate syrup on it. As the film was in black and white they didn't have to worry about blood not looking real.

(587) The Texas Chainsaw Massacre 2 bombed at the box-office. It opened around the same time as The Fly remake but The Fly did much better both in terms of box-office and reviews.

(588) Ben Mendelsohn was nearly cast as Pennywise in the big screen version of IT.

(589) The Babadook was called The Pages of Horror in Greece.

(590) The studio who purchased Paranormal Activity initially planned to remake it with a bigger budget and leave the original unreleased.

(591) Patrick Stewart called Lifeforce the nadir of his career.

(592) Kirsten Dunst was going to be in Final Destination at one point but was replaced by Ali Larter.

(593) 4bia (aka Phobia) is a 2008 Thai anthology horror film directed by Youngyooth Thongkonthun, Banjong

Pisanthanakun, Parkpoom Wongpoom, and Paween Purijitpanya. This is a stylish and pretty good anthology that is worth a look if you love compendium horror films. 4bia is a very stylish and competent anthology on the whole. None of the segments will knock your socks off but all of them are interesting. Modern horror anthologies can be a bit hit or miss but this is an example of one that works. It feels a very traditional sort of film too despite being a 21st century anthology and maybe that's a big part of its success. There's no found footage stuff or over the top tongue-in-cheek shenanigans. It's just a very well made little chiller.

(594) Jamie Lee Curtis named the forgotten 1999 science fiction horror picture Virus as the worst film she's ever been involved in.

(595) Veronica Lake was one of Hollywood's biggest stars in the 1940s with her long (and much imitated) 'peek-a-boo' hair. Her films included This Gun for Hire, The Hour Before Dawn, Hold That Blonde, and Out of this World. However, her life was to have a strange and sad final act in relative obscurity. She suffered from schizophrenia and alcoholism and only made two (forgotten horror) films after 1952. In the 1960s a journalist found her working as a waitress in a cheap New York hotel. Lake's drinking had ravaged her once stunning looks and she became unrecognisable from the stylish Hollywood star of the 1940s. Lake now looked bloated and prematurely aged. She wasn't taking care of herself. Lake's last film, and her first for 22 years, was 1970's Flesh Feast.

This horror film is regarded to be one of the worst movies ever made. It's a cheapjack oddity where the cast flub their lines but the camera keeps rolling. Lake plays a mad scientist who ends up torturing Hitler by putting maggots on his face. Lake looked like a homeless bag lady in the film and it was hard to believe she was once the most glamorous woman in Hollywood. Lake was married several times but none of the marriages seemed to last. She published a memoir in the 1970s in a vague attempt to boost her defunct career but it didn't seem to do much for her. She was suffering from hepatitis and in 1973 entered hospital where staff were surprised that Lake - once such an icon of Hollywood - never seemed to have any guests or visitors. Acute renal failure set in and she died in 1973. Her modest funeral was paid for by her ghostwriter. Her son had to take out a loan to claim the body and have her cremated. Lake's third husband had refused to lend any money to him. Unbelievably, Lake's ashes remained in the funeral home until 1976 because no one stumped up the expenses to take them. Legend (and possibly urban myth) has it that Veronica Lake's ashes ended up in a curiosity shop in New York.

(596) Michael Winslow, the sound effects officer in Police Academy, provided some of the voices for Gremlins.

(597) Ellen Burstyn chose to duck out of the Exorcist sequel. Linda Blair obviously couldn't afford to be so picky.

(598) A criminally underrated remake is Chuck Russell's 1988 version of The Blob. This film is a lot of fun and also genuinely scary at times.

(599) There was only actually one cube room on the set of the 1997 film Cube. They just constantly changed the colours to make it seem like the characters were making their way through different rooms.

(600) Joseph Pilato, who played Captain Rhodes, was annoyed that he was one of the few cast members in George Romero's Day of the Dead who didn't get to go to Florida to shoot the film's opening scenes.

(601) The refrigerated bedroom set on The Exorcist was cooled with four air conditioners and temperatures would plunge to around 30 to 40 below zero. It was so cold that perspiration would freeze on some of the cast and crew.

(602) The 1985 comedy film Teen Wolf was a bit hit and

carried along by the comic charisma of a young Michael J Fox.
A few years later a sequel was made - this time directed by
Christopher Leitch. Michael J Fox clearly had better things to
do with his time by now as Back to the Future had made him a
big star. He is replaced in the sequel by Jason Bateman (who
was a child and teen star in addition to the successful career he
went on to enjoy as an adult). Bateman plays the cousin of
Fox's character, a teenager named Todd who is also afflicted
with the werewolf gene. Scott, much like Fox in the first film,
discovers that being a werewolf has more than its fair share of
perks. It gives you amazing athletic abilities and makes you
popular with girls. So it is then that Scott is dragooned into the
school boxing team because of his amazing werewolf powers.
However, he starts to wonder if he has sight of his real self -
arrogant as he has become with his popular werewolf antics.

Teen Wolf has been largely forgotten these days so you can
only imagine how low profile this inferior sequel must be now.
It drew dreadful reviews (Siskel & Ebert were famously harsh)
and remains a complete and utter waste of time for both the
viewer and anyone who has ever bothered to sit through it.
Only a few supporting characters from the first film return and
Teen Wolf Too has hardly a film that cried out for a sequel
anyway. The joke was probably just about exhausted by the
first film. Did we really need to have more of this? Teen Wolf
Too is a poorly written unfunny cash grab with nothing to
recommend it. Bateman proves to be a poor substitute for Fox
and he's saddled with a far weaker film too. This is a very poor
sequel that is best avoided.

(603) At the end of "The Lonesome Death Of Jordy Verrill" in
George Romero's anthology horror film Creepshow, the sign
post points to Castle Rock. Castle Rock is the fictional town
where many of Stephen Kings' stories take place

(604) Apollo 18 is a 2011 horror film directed by Gonzalo
López-Gallego. The premise is that the cancelled Apollo 18
mission actually landed on the Moon but encountered aliens.
This is a found footage film but not one of the better ones.

Apollo 18 is too slow for its own good and is only really recommended for those who don't mind a slow burn horror. There's a decent sense of atmosphere at times and the grainy footage is quite well done. The aliens seem to be disguised as rocks and look like crab spiders when we get a glimpse of them in a clear homage to the facehugger.

(605) The first Purge film was very cheap to make but grossed $89 million. It became a very profitable franchise.

(606) In order to save money, the Hammer horror films would scout locations within walking distance of the studio.

(607) Michael Crichton became inspired to write the original Westworld after a trip to Disneyland, where he saw the Pirates of the Caribbean ride, and was impressed by the animatronic characters. "I make up little stories about how I get ideas, but I really don't know most of the time. I think I got the idea for Westworld because I was very interested in the astronauts. I was fascinated by the fact they were being trained to be machines. Then I was also fascinated by the animated figures at Disneyland. The two tendencies toward making people as machine like as possible and machines as human as possible are creating a lot of confusion. That's what suggested Westworld to me. The tendency to make concessions to machines can only grow. Zip codes, for example, are a concession to machines. There are advantages and disadvantages to this tendency. I don't think that people are strongly threatened by zip codes; it's inevitable that we accommodate ourselves to the machines we need to support our existence."

(608) David Fincher was only 28 years-old when he directed Alien 3.

(609) Tippi Hedren claimed that the scene in The Birds where her character is besieged by crazed birds was shot for days by Hitchcock and he deliberately got glass on her face as revenge for spurning his advances.

(610) Oddly enough, considering it got very good reviews, The Blair Witch Project was nominated for a Razzie as worst picture!

(611) Joss Whedon and Drew Goddard wrote The Cabin in the Woods in only three days.

(612) George Romero's Dawn of the Dead took four months to shoot.

(613) The child who plays Newt's brother Timmy in the Aliens director's cut scenes on LV-426 is Carrie Henn's real life brother.

(614) The gardens of comedian Harold Lloyd's estate were used for some of the amusement park sequences in the original Westworld film.

(615) While Hammer films were considered rather bold in the fifties, by the seventies they were starting to look a bit twee and dated, especially in comparison to the American horror revival of the sixties and seventies that brought films like The Excorcist, Night of the Living Dead and The Texas Chainsaw Massacre. They even faced competition from home with Amicus, a British studio that carved out a niche with contemporary horror anthology films laced with famous guest stars.

(616) Frank Darabont originally wanted his adaption of Stephen King's The Mist to be a black and white film.

(617) The period the 2014 horror film It Follows takes place in is deliberately vague to make the film seem off-kilter and strange. Some of the technology in the film seems modern but the characters also have cathode ray televisions that show old films.

(618) Ethan Hawke turned down the role of Josh Lambert in Insidious.

(619) It is never really explained in the Purge movies why people don't just go abroad for a few days to avoid the Purge night violence. Maybe the totalitarian government in the movie bans citizens from leaving during the Purge?

(620) John Carpenter once said that inferior remakes of his classic films don't bother him because he gets some money each time they do one.

(621) Bela Lugosi never wore fangs when he played Dracula.

(622) The transformation scene in the 1941 film The Wolf Man took ten hours to film.

(623) Dracula has been played over 2,000 times by various actors.

(624) Wes Craven never envisioned A Nightmare On Elm Street as a potential franchise. A slew of sequels followed though.

(625) There are no exterior shots in the first Saw movie because they couldn't afford to shoot any.

(626) Eddie Murphy was apparently under consideration for the villain in Candyman. It's hard to imagine that anyone could have done a better job than Tony Todd though.

(627) The Stuff is an enjoyable if uneven satirical horror film directed by Larry Cohen. A gloopy white substance that is similar to ice cream is found in a hole in the ground (rather silly the way a man notices the stuff and tastes it, it could be chemical waste for all he knows!) and soon becomes a sensation when sold in supermarkets. Consumers report that it makes them feel great and it also doesn't seem to have any calories. Food manufacturers hire an industrial spy (the great Michael Moriarty) to investigate the 'Stuff' that's putting them out of business. Turns out the Stuff might not be harmless as it seems. This film has great fun spoofing commercials of the era

and gets a lot of juice from Moriarty as the sassy investigator. It transpires that the Stuff, when consumed, seems to take over people, sometimes rendering them violent. The gloopy white substance eats you just as much as you eat it and is very much alive. There are some effective moments of horror in the film but Cohen seems just as concerned with the need to keep the jokes coming.

(628) Gargoyles was directed by Bill L Norton from a screenplay by Stephen and Elinor Karpf. This tv film is fondly remembered by those who caught it as youngsters and features FX by the great Stan Winston. The premise has a professor (played by Cornel Wilde) of occult literature running into (gulp) gargoyles while on a trip to the desert to investigate a strange skeleton. He and his daughter (played by Jennifer Salt) are soon up their neck in gargoyle trouble. This is a very enjoyable tv film that runs to about 75 minutes. The isolated backdrop is perfect for the story with plenty of cave capers and Bernie Casey's chief gargoyle is memorable for his commanding voice and unhealthy interest in Jennifer Salt.

The scares are not bad at all with a bed sequence especially good and plenty of clawed jumps. The gargoyles are well realised too. Look at Casey's strikingly intricate make-up. By the way, this film must surely have been an influence on Jeepers Creepers. Casey's winged gargoyle is rather similar to the creeper monster. Look out for Scott Glenn in one of the supporting roles.

(629) Piranha II: The Spawning is a 1981 Italian horror film and the sequel to Joe Dante's cult classic Piranha. James Cameron (yes, THAT James Cameron) is the credited director but he says he didn't have much to do with the film. "I was replaced after two-and-a-half weeks by the Italian producer," said Cameron. "He just fired me and took over, which is what he wanted to do when he hired me. It wasn't until much later that I even figured out what had happened. It was like, 'Oh, man, I thought I was doing a good job.' But when I saw what they were cutting together, it was horrible. And then the

producer wouldn't take my name off the picture because [contractually] they couldn't deliver it with an Italian name. So they left me on, no matter what I did. I had no legal power to influence him from Pomona, California, where I was sleeping on a friend's couch. I didn't even know an attorney. In actual fact, I did some directing on the film, but I don't feel it was my first movie." Cameron has said that he considers The Terminator to be his real directorial debut.

Piranha II: The Spawning is a famously daft film that has piranhas menacing a West Indian holiday resort. But that's not even the half of it. Oh no. These piranhas are especially deadly because they can fly! Piranha II: The Spawning is a silly cheapjack film that really suffers without Joe Dante. Did you know by the way that Steven Spielberg personally handpicked Dante to direct Gremlins because Piranha was his favourite Jaws rip-off? The special effects are laughably bad in the film with the killer fish looking patently fake and silly as they 'fly' through the air. The only interesting thing about the film is an appearance by Lance Henriksen, an actor who would go on to become a cult genre star in sci-fi and horror. Piranha II: The Spawning might be good for a laugh or two but the film is rather boring at times and not the best example of a 'so bad its good' film. As a sequel though this is obviously a complete disaster.

(630) At the wrap party for Hellraiser, Doug Bradley found that some of the crew didn't know who he was because they'd only ever seen him made-up as Pinhead.

(631) Ronald Shusett and Dan O'Bannon's original (and remarkably modest - given what Alien would become) plan was for the screenplay to be a Roger Corman film. If anyone could get Star Beast (the original title of Alien) made it was bargain basement maestro Roger Corman. The budget would be small but the film would get made. However, before Shusett and O'Bannon signed a contract with Corman, a man named Mark Haggard (of Goldwyn Studios) asked to read the screenplay and was intrigued enough to pass it on to Walter

Hill and David Giler - two writers who apparently had the ear
and the "confidence" of Fox executive Alan Ladd. Jr

(632) In the original ending to Fright Night, Roddy
McDowall's character was going to turn into a vampire live on
air while hosting his horror show.

(633) The Craft is a 1996 film about four teenage outcast girls
who dabble in witchcraft to make themselves more popular
and get what they want but, as ever in the horror genre, you
should be careful what you wish for. Angelina Jolie auditioned
to be in this movie but didn't get a part.

(634) Tom Atkins, who plays the mean dad in the prologue of
Creepshow, wanted to play Jordy Verrill but that part had
already been promised to Stephen King.

(635) Glenn Close and Melanie Griffith auditioned for the part
of Carrie White in Brian DePalma's film.

(636) Bordello of Blood is the second spin-off film from the
HBO Tales from the Crypt series. Stephen Baldwin left at the
last minute and was replaced by comedian Dennis Miller.
A good chunk of the budget was used to pay Miller's $1 million
salary. Corey Feldman hated working with Dennis Miller on
this movie and said Miller was a 'dick' to the cast and crew.

(637) George Romero's 1973 film The Crazies (which got a so-
so remake years later) is set in and around the small town of
Evans City, Pennsylvania, where a plane transporting a secret
military biological weapon/virus (code-named 'Trixie') crashes
with terrible consequences for the local inhabitants. The virus
enters the water supply and begins to gradually turn many of
the civilians violent and crazed as panic and confusion rises.
The Crazies is a thoughtful and interesting slice of horror only
hampered by the modest budget and the sometimes
rudimentary nature of the film.

(638) Found footage was by no means a new idea even in 1999

but the unexpected success of Blair Witch seemed to thrust this subgenre into the mainstream.

(639) Pasta, milk and marbles were used to depict the insides of the android Ash in Alien.

(640) The War Of The Worlds is one of the most famous and influential science fiction novels ever written. It first appeared in 1898 and remains the main inspiration for the numerous alien invasion themed films and television shows that have followed through the years. The story appeared at a time when Giovanni Schiaparelli's discovery of Martian canals and Percival Lowell's book Mars created speculation that there could actually be intelligent life on the Red Planet. The War of the Worlds is told in the first person by a narrator who is a perfectly normal and respectable Victorian gentleman living in sleepy Surrey.

The book is related as his (almost journalistic) account of the extraordinary events of several years ago. The opening conveys much scientific information about Mars (Wells did have a background in science) as the narrator meets with an astronomer friend of his named Ogilvy and is intrigued by the stories of strange lights and gases coming from the Red Planet. 'The chances of anything man-like on Mars are a million to one,' the astronomer reassures him. Ogilvy is wrong though as the unfortunate inhabitants of London will soon discover. There soon comes the first 'falling star'. Huge and mysterious metal cylinders begin to crash land on commons and in woods around London. Humanity, or rather good old Blighty, is in for a very nasty surprise. Despite himself, the narrator is terribly excited by all the events and talk of men from Mars but considers it something of a shame that these poor creatures are liable to be either dead already or a sitting duck for the military authorities to destroy with shells should they so choose to. It doesn't seem fair somehow. The sleepy, languid summer atmosphere set up by Wells is shattered when the Martians emerge from their cylinders and pits in huge mechanical tripods armed with a terrifying 'heat ray' weapon.

Soon the narrator is caught up in the panic and joins the refugees as the apparently unstoppable Martians lay waste to everything around them in destructive fashion.

(641) Plans to make feature films about the Moors Murders (believe it or not the American film director William Friedkin was once attached to a Moors Murders film) and the Yorkshire Ripper were shelved in the end because they were deemed too controversial.

(642) Ravenous is a cult 1999 Western horror film about cannibalism. The film stars Guy Pearce and Robert Carlyle and is worth watching if you've never seen it before.

(643) Joss Whedon wrote a third act for Alien Resurrection involving a battle on earth and also various multiple endings. None of them were shot for the actual film.

(644) In her memoir, the daughter of Vincent Price said that her legendary father was a big fan of rollercoasters!

(645) George Romero was supposed to direct the first Resident Evil film but was thrown off the project when his script was deemed too uncommercial.

(646) Quentin Tarantino said his favourite 80s slasher film is the 1981 Canadian movie My Bloody Valentine.

(647) The producer Dino De Laurentiis allegedly rejected Meryl Streep for the lead role in his King Kong remake because he didn't think she was good looking enough. Jessica Lange was another matter entirely and he cast her immediately.

(648) One complaint some fans have with the director's cut of Aliens is that they feel the colony scenes on LV-426 diminish the tension because we now know what has happened before the marines arrive. It's a reasonable nitpick although, to be honest, even without these scenes we sort of already know

what happened anyway. The xenomorphs happened! One could perhaps argue that the Hadley's Hope colony scenes could be trimmed somewhat in the director's cut but it's fun anyway to see Newt 'before' and what a lung busting scream from Carrie Henn at the facehugger reveal!

(649) The Wicker Tree is a 2011 sequel to 1973's The Wicker Man - both directed by Robin Hardy. The Wicker Man is generally regarded to be one of the greatest British horror films ever made. This wretched sequel is an amateurish waste of everyone's time. Hardy based The Wicker Tree on his novel Cowboys for Christ. The ludicrous story has two young American Christians named Steve (Henry Garrett) and Beth Boothby (Britannia Nicol) sent to 'heathen' Scotland to teach them about God. They end up being invited to a village by Sir Lachlan Morrison (Graham McTavish) and, well, if you've seen the original film, you'll have a good idea of what eventually happens. Nothing in this terrible film makes much sense and it's little wonder that it didn't find a theatrical release. The notion that Scotland is some primitive backwater is preposterous for a film made in 2011. You'd think Hardy would know better.

The two American leads can't act to save their lives and the film plays like cheap student film shot with a camcorder. Most of the actors here seem embarrassed and aware that they've ended up in a real stinker. Christopher Lee was going to be the lead of the film but had to pull out because of illness. Lucky for him really. He has a cameo instead with the lead villain role going to Graham McTavish. What this film illustrates perfectly is how the original Wicker Man was lightning in a bottle. You just can't replicate the wonderfully strange and chilling nature of that 'folk horror' film. Robin Hardy (who hardly made any films in between these two Wicker Man pictures) should really have left The Wicker Man to stand alone as an undoubted classic of British cinema. If you do love the original it is best to pretend that The Wicker Tree doesn't exist.

(650) The Legend of Boggy Creek is a horror docudrama about

the "Fouke Monster", a Bigfoot-type creature that has been
seen in and around Fouke, Arkansas since the 1950s. The film
mixes staged interviews with some local residents who claim
to have encountered the creature, along with fictitious
reenactments of said encounters. Charles B Pierce, an
advertising salesman from Texarkana on the Arkansas/Texas
border, borrowed over $100,000 from a local trucking
company, used an old 35mm movie camera and hired locals
(mainly high school students) to help make the 90-minute
film. This docudrama is not to be taken very seriously but it's
enjoyably strange and compelling with the very 1970s
atmosphere and nature montages. You even get a couple of
songs thrown into the mix. The basic structure of The Legend
of Boggy Creek is that around the endless montages of
woodland and shots of rivers, you get encounters with the
monster recreated in the docudrama style. Docudramas are
very commonplace now but I'd imagine they were more of a
novelty in 1972.

You get amateurish re-enactments of people being spooked in
their houses mostly. It's all quite effective and spooky at times.
This film was apparently a big influence on The Blair Witch
Project with its rough and ready style. My favourite moment
occurs when a man is frightened by the monster while on the
toilet and when he jumps up he still has his undergarments on.
That's a very strange way of going to the toilet I must say.

(651) The Italian zombie film Zombi 2 was falsely marketed as
a sequel to George Romero's Dawn of the Dead. The director
Lucio Fulci said he had nothing to do with this brazen
commercial ploy.

(652) The character of Patrick Bateman in the Bret Easton
Ellis book (and later film) American Pyscho clearly owes a lot
to Ted Bundy.

(653) Galaxy of Terror is a 1981 science fiction horror film
produced by Roger Corman and directed by Bruce D Clark.
This is another in the slew of Alien copycats that followed in

the wake of Ridley Scott's classic. Galaxy of Terror is very low budget but it does have some things going for it. James Cameron worked on the special effects and designs and the cast is not bad at all. It includes Sid Haig and a young Robert Englund. Despite the small budget the film is quite effective in depicting a storm raged planet of nightmares and the deaths are rather gruesome when they arrive. Erin Moran (of the sitcom Happy Days and its spin-off Joanie Loves Chachi) meets a most brutal end and Taaffe O'Connell is raped by a gigantic maggot. This was a pretty controversial scene because Taaffe's character seems to be quite enjoying her demise. Personally, I can think of better ways to go.

(654) In 1995, Tales the Crypt made the jump to the big screen with Demon Knight (aka Tales from the Crypt Presents: Demon Knight). The story of Tales from the Crypt's jump to the big screen is complicated and confusing and full of fascinating what might have beens. It seems to be fairly common knowledge that Peter Jackson's The Frighteners and Quentin Tarantino and Robert Rodriguez's From Dusk Till Dawn both could have been Tales from the Crypt movies. At some early embryonic stage both were planned to head this way.

From Dusk Till Dawn in particular seems like a perfect fit for Tales from the Crypt with its jumbling of gore, humour, and bawdiness. From Dusk Till Dawn was supposed to follow Demon Knight but Tarantino and Rodriguez fell out with the Crypt producers and took their film elsewhere. The Frighteners was developed by Peter Jackson for Robert Zemeckis. Zemeckis planned to direct the film as a Crypt spin-off but he was so impressed by the screenplay he insisted that Jackson should make the film himself.

(655) Ridley Scott's Prometheus doesn't have that Planet of the Vampires desolate mist shrouded atmosphere we associate with the Alien franchise. These characters don't look like they are on an alien world. They look like they are in Iceland!

(656) Drew Barrymore's early death in Scream was clever misdirection as some viewers expected her to be a major character.

(657) The fantastical and creepy monster designs seen in the outlandish films of director Guillermo del Toro were a big influence on the Demogorgon in Stranger Things.

(658) The mediocre 2009 horror film Berdella starred Seth Correa as the infamous Bob Berdella. Robert Andrew Berdella was born in 1949, in Cuyahoga Falls, Ohio. Berdella was a serial killer who restrained, tortured, and killed at least six men from 1984 to 1987 in Kansas City, Missouri. He was known as The Kansas City Butcher. Berdella was said to be rather aloof and detached as a child. He had a brother who he always felt overshadowed by because his brother was athletic and good at sport while he wasn't. Berdella was quite dumpy and wore thick glasses. Berdella deduced he was gay from a very young age but he struggled to come to terms with his sexuality and didn't admit to it for a long time. As a teenager he even had a few girlfriends in an attempt to disguise his real self. His father died when he was a relatively young man and this is said to have made him even more aloof and withdrawn. Berdella didn't like the fact that his mother then remarried. Berdella's hobbies were collecting stamps, strange art, and antiques.

In the early eighties he used his collection to start a business. Berdella ran a booth at a market called Bob's Bizarre Bizarre which sold oddities and antiques. It is sometimes suggested that he might sold some of the skulls of his victims at this booth. Berdella studied art at college but dropped out in the end. During this period he was busted on drugs charges a few times. One of the drugs he used was the mind altering LSD.

Despite this, Berdella seemed - on the outside - to be doing quite well. He was popular in the community in which he lived and, in addition to the business he started, got work as a chef. Berdella seemed to befriend a lot of runaways and male prostitutes. He claimed to be a sort of mentor to them and said he was helping them with drug addictions. The police later deduced that Berdella wasn't quite so generous as he claimed in his relationships with these young men. They believe he was exploiting them for sex. By now, Berdella was pretty open about his sexuality and most people he knew were aware that he was gay. Berdella murdered for the first time in 1984. His victims were all young men that he had gained the trust of and then isolated. The murders were very sadistic - even for a serial killer. Berdella would drug and restrain the victims and then basically torture them for as long as they could suvive. The victims were raped, cut, given electric shocks, and he would even inject them with cleaning fluids in the neck so they couldn't scream. Berdella would often the break the bones of the victims' hands with an iron bar so that they couldn't put up a struggle.

Berdella claimed to have been influenced by the 1965 film The Collector (which adapted a novel by John Fowles) - where an alienated young man is obsessed by a female student and makes her a captive in his cellar. He wanted his victims to become compliant and trust him. However, most of them died from torture long before they got anywhere near this stage. Berdella's disturbing activities came to an end in 1988 when a male prostitute named Christopher Bryson, after days of torture, managed to escape from Berdella's home and run across the street (in a dog collar). He found some police and told them what had happened. The badly injured Bryson was taken to hospital and the police eventually obtained permission to search Berdella's home. They found that he had an elaborate torture room but the worst was yet to come. They also found human skulls and a human head. There was a chainsaw covered in human blood and various body parts. The police also found photographs Berdella had taken of his victims in various stages of torture. Berdella had also written detailed diaries of his torture methods. Berdella was sentenced to life imprisonment without the possibility of parole. He had to do a plea bargain to avoid the death penalty. This involved a full confession in order to help identify all of his victims.

Berdella was the worst sort of serial killer in that he was more interested in torture than death. He would keep his victims alive as long as he could before he killed them or they died. Berdella never seemed to express much remorse for his terrible crimes. When he was in prison he complained that the authorities witheld his medication for high blood pressure. He died of a heart attack in 1992 at the age of 43. It's safe to say that no one had much sympathy when they heard he had died. When the judge at Berdella's trial heard the killer had died in prison, he is reported to have smiled and said - "Couldn't have happened to a nicer guy."

(659) Damien Thorn was originally going to die at the end of The Omen but they obviously changed this because they wanted a sequel.

(660) Hostel was shot at an abandoned mental hospital in Prague.

(661) Friday the 13th was originally going to be called Long Night at Camp Blood.

(662) Bruce Campbell said that after the income tax people, an ex-wife, and agents and managers had taken their slice he ended up with peanuts for his role in Army of Darkness.

(663) Tobe Hooper was the director of the classic 1982 horror film Poltergeist. This film was written and produced by Steven Spielberg and stories persist that he secretly directed most of it. Spielberg was prepping E.T at the time and his studio contract forbode him from directing another film. This is why he asked Texas Chainsaw Massacre director Tobe Hooper to direct his Poltergeist script. Spielberg was on the set of Poltergeist a lot and later seemed to suggest he had made all the major decisions because Tobe Hopper wasn't a 'take charge' sort of person. Spielberg later had to apologise to Hooper in The Hollywood Reporter for suggesting that he (Spielberg) had made the film himself. The stories that Spielberg secretly directed Poltergeist stem a lot by comments

by Zelda Rubenstein - one of the stars of the film. Rubenstein said that Spielberg had directed all the scenes she took part in. Rubenstein also said that Hooper was out of his head on drugs during her time on the set. Other actors in the cast have disputed Rubenstein's account and defended Tobe Hooper. Whatever the actual truth, Poltergeist feels an awful lot like a Steven Spielberg film at times. If any film feels like Dark Amblin it is surely Poltergeist.

(664) It was Chris Sarandon's idea for his vampire in Fright Night to be constantly eating apples. This is because certain types of bats love fruit.

(665) Jack Nicholson used to be a volunteer firefighter and so had no trouble smashing a door with an axe in The Shining.

(666) The 2009 film Slaughter was inspired by Belle Gunness. Belle Gunness was a Norwegian woman who moved to the United States in 1881. She married a fellow Norwegian and they ran a store together. They had four children, two of whom died young. By the turn of the century the store had burned down - claiming the life of Belle's husband. She used the insurance payout to buy a farm in Indiana. Belle married another man but this second marriage only lasted several moths before he was found dead. She claimed he had been struck by a meat grinder by accident and - evidence to the contrary elusive - an investigation ruled out any suspicion of foul play. Belle began searching for a third husband by placing adverts in local newspapers. She stipulated that anyone interested in the ads would have to come to the farm in Indiana to meet her. Several men made the trip but all of them vanished without trace thereafter. There was clearly something of the night about Belle Gunness. This was a woman it was best to avoid - if you wanted to live that is.

In 1908, a fire broke out at the farm and caused much damage. There were some grisly secrets uncovered by the blaze. The remains of Belle's surviving children were found - in addition to the headless body of a woman. The authorities searched for the head and found the remains of several men who had visited the farm in response to Belle's newspaper ad. There were eleven victims in all. At this point the story of Belle Gunness becomes mysterious. The authorities suspected the headless body to be Belle Gunness but her fate remains unknown. There were many alleged sightings of her in the following years. Ray Lamphere, a farmhand who had worked for Belle and might have been a lover, was suspected of the murders but only charged with arson. It is possible that he conspired with Gunness to lure the men to the farm where they could be killed and robbed. Could it be that Belle had faked her own death in order to escape? A fire would seem as good a way as any to do that. The strange and confusing legend of Belle Gunness quickly grew. The farm became a rather dark sort of tourist attraction and her name would forever be inked to chilling tales of murder and crime.

(667) HP Lovecraft (1890-1937) was an American horror writer best known for creating the Cthulhu Mythos. The theme of Lovecraft's work was that of an indifferent and unfathomable universe that mankind can never hope to understand. The universe is full of monstrous ancient creatures and dark secret places. If we ever encountered the truth that underpins our reality in Lovecraft's work we would go insane. Madness threatened with Lovecraft's pantheon of Elder Things and his rather bleak take on the universe. A vast random harrowing place without any spiritual meaning where man is inconsequential. Memorable Lovecraft inspired films include re-Animator and In the Mouth of Madness.

(668) Prince of Darkness is John Carpenter paying homage to British writer Nigel Kneale - who was famous for his frequent fusion of science and the supernatural. The basic premise is that Satan is a gloop of green slime in a basement and attempting to take human form but Carpenter's plot and explanations eventually go way beyond this into anti-matter, aliens, Jesus, and TACHYON messages from the future.

(669) The crew on The Evil Dead burned the cabin furniture to

stay warm because it was very cold when they shot the film. (670) Event Horizon is 1997 sci-fi horror film directed by the much maligned Paul WS Anderson. You could make a solid case for this being the best film that Anderson has directed. The film is about an expedition to find a missing ship called 'Event Horizon' which has suddenly re-appeared near Neptune. It transpires that the Event Horizon had experimental engine technology and when it was activated it may have warped into another dimension. The crew of the ship mutilated each other and all went insane. Could it be that the Event Horizon opened a portal to Hell? Event Horizon started life as much more of an Alien homage but the final script pivoted it towards Hellraiser too so some of the pure Alien DNA was lost. It's still clearly a film that loves the Alien franchise though and the gothic elements vaguely evoke Alien 3. What links Event Horizon and Alien is the intent to make a haunted house film in space.

There's a great cast here too with Laurence Fishburne, Sam Neil, Jason Isaacs, Kathleen Quinlan, and Joely Richardson. Event horizon is a decent horror space thriller and one of the few Paul WS Anderson films that you would actually encourage people to watch.

(671) Wes Craven's 1977 film The Hills Have Eyes, about a family who get lost in the desert and run into murderous cannibal mutants affected by nuclear testing, was well regarded and inspired a remake many years later. 1984's The Hills Have Eyes Part II has no excuses because it was made by Craven himself. He later disowned the sequel and said he only made it because he was desperate for money (this was presumably just before A Nightmare On Elm street became a big hit for Craven). Craven apparently abandoned The Hills Have Eyes Part II before it was finished but was persuaded to go back and complete it - purely for the money. It is very apparent watching the film that Craven never shot much footage and didn't have much interest in the film. Why? Well, because huge swathes of this sequel are padded out with flashback footage from the first film! It doesn't exactly make

you feel as if you are getting value for money. One flashback is famously supposed to be that of a dog!

(672) Ridley Scott said his intention with Alien was to make a 'vicious $10 million B-movie'.

(673) The role of Father Malone in John Carpenter's The Fog was offered to Christopher Lee.

(674) Science fiction writer Harlan Ellison took legal action against Orion Pictures when he saw The Terminator. James Cameron had heavily borrowed from Ellison's Outer Limits episode 'Soldier' and Orion were ordered to include an acknowledgement of Ellison in the credits. in the Outer Limits episode (which is set eighteen hundred years in the future) two soldiers fight in a desolate smoke hazed landscape of rubble and destruction before two beams of light suddenly appear and hurl them into a time vortex. One of them, Qarlo Clobregnny (Michael Ansara), suddenly finds himself hurled back to 1964 and lands on a city street where his sudden appearance (he's wearing armour, an anachronistic steel helmet and has a ray gun!) is highly alarming to the population as you can imagine. Qarlo is the ultimate soldier. He is eventually restrained and thrown in a lunatic asylum (the "G.I.C.D. Psychiatric Security Section") but a philologist named Tom Kagan (Lloyd Nolan) manages to establish a connection to Qarlo and starts to "tame" him of his aggressive tendencies and conditioning. However, the other futuristic soldier (Alan Jaffe) appears in 1964 too and is intent on hunting down Qarlo.

(675) Night of the Demon is a 1957 British horror film directed by Jacques Tourneur and based on the MR James story Casting the Runes. This is a wonderfully atmospheric little thriller that masterfully uses suspense and the power of suggestion to camouflage its modest budget. The producer was responsible for chopping ten minutes from the film and retitling it Curse of the Demon for the American release. You should really watch the longer version as the deliberate and

sedate pacing of Night of the Demon is one of its charms.
(676) The Abominable Dr Phibes was directed by Robert Fuest
and written by William Goldstein and James Whiton. Dr
Anton Phibes (Vincent Price) is a brilliant scholar and organist
who was presumed dead in a 1921 car crash which killed his
wife (played by Caroline Munro). It turns out that Phibes is
not dead. He's very much alive although badly injured and
now wears a prosthetic mask and can only speak through an
electrical voice device. Phibes seeks revenge against the
doctors he blames for not saving his beloved wife and plans to
kill them using the ten plagues of Egypt as his inspiration. The
Abominable Dr Phibes is one of the best cult horror films of
the seventies and a fantastically bizarre and stylish experience.
Very rarely will you see a modestly budgeted horror film look
so fantastic.

(677) The underground scenes in 1981's My Bloody Valentine
were shot in a real Canadian mine.

(678) For the scene in The Texas Chainsaw Massacre where
Leatherface is cut by the chainsaw, Gunnar Hansen wore a
metal plate on his leg for protection.

(679) Threads is a BAFTA award winning television film
written by Barry Hines and directed by Mick Jackson. Threads
is one of the most harrowing dramas ever to appear on British
television. Threads depicts a nuclear strike on Britain through
the prism of ordinary people in the city of Sheffield. Half the
country is wiped out, millions die, there is blindness and
radiation sickness, society collapses, and the pathetic survivors
find themselves living in a grim new Stone Age. Threads is
terrifying and sobering as it should be. This is no Hollywood
depiction of nuclear war but a very real seeming ground level
look at the consequences of the unthinkable happening. It was
made at a time when Cold War tensions were very much a part
of the news. It's little wonder that it greatly affected those who
saw it. Not only was Threads harrowing but it depicted an
event that could conceivably happen. Like The War Game,
Threads makes a mockery of government 'how to survive'

materials of the era. The government would be woefully unprepared for what would really happen and those who did somehow survive would find themselves in something akin to hell on earth. Threads has a chilling final coda but all of it is chilling and it remains one of the most unsettling things ever broadcast on television.

(680) Steven Spielberg came up with the ending of Paranormal Activity because he felt the original idea wasn't scary enough.

(681) David Hedison said that the original scene of Andre trapped in the spider's web in 1958's The Fly was scarier because it was his own voice. He says they altered it to make him sound more 'chipmunk' like and he disliked that.

(682) Actor Kris Lemche spent two days learning to drive a forklift truck for the scene in the hardware store in Final Destination 2.

(683) Nineteen Eighty-Four was first published in 1949 and is one of those novels that still feels topical decades after it was published. A number of terms in the novel (like Big Brother, Thought Police, and Room 101) have entered the general lexicon and are still used today. Nineteen Eighty-Four concerns Winston Smith, an everyman worker bee living in a totalitarian state known as Oceania. Britain, where Smith lives, is now called Airstrip One and part of Oceania. There are three huge superstates which now control the world but news is so censored and controlled that few ordinary people have much idea of what is actually going on. They are told there is a constant war happening somewhere and their work lives revolve around the Party - which is headed by the mysterious and cult like Big Brother. Life is pretty grim in this totalitarian society and few people can even remember what things were like before the Party seized control. Workers are involved in tasks like editing old newspapers and changing novels to make history conform to the present. No dissent or free thought is tolerated - which is bad news for Winston Smith because he is

starting to question this society and system. He is also in danger of falling in love (which, outside of marriage, is forbidden in this society).

Nineteen Eighty-Four is one of the most influential novels of the 20th Century. Literally every dystopian science fiction film you've ever watched has borrowed from this book and it's not too difficult to see certain parallels with some of the themes and concepts of Nineteen Eighty-Four in our surveillance obsessed governments and the rather dubious nature of much of the news we receive. Orwell's totalitarian society in the novel is based on Stalin's version of the Soviet Union - which practiced a far more sinister, deadly, and undemocractic form of socialism than the one Orwell wanted. Orwell's general warning though was that all political systems should be watched carefully lest they begin to flirt with any totalitarian concepts.

(684) Elfen Lied is a manga series and later anime. Elfen Lied is about a mutant 'Diclonius' girl named Lucy who has telekinetic powers and escapes from a military facility. It has some very obvious parallels with Stranger Things and was cited as one of the influences by the creators of the show.

(685) When they made a Hollywood film version of Alan Moore's brilliant graphic novel From Hell, Moore was especially annoyed that his sarcastic and world weary London detective Frederick Abberline was turned into an absthine swigging Johnny Depp!

(686) In 1967, the Carry On comedy films spoofed Hammer Studios to good effect in Carry On Screaming. While the Carry Ons are generally remembered as being cheap and cheerful (and I suppose many of them were in their own charming way) we shouldn't forget the craft and invention that went into the historical capers and Carry On Screaming serves as an impressive pastiche of Hammer and horror films in general with great cinematography, plenty of atmosphere, and some wonderful sets and costumes. The monsters (which include

riffs on The Mummy, Frankenstein's Monster and Vampires) are a lot of fun too. Sid James was unavailable to film this one and was replaced by Steptoe & Son star Harry H Corbett (in what would be his only Carry On). Corbett makes a nice addition to the team here and works very well with Peter Butterworth as a comical Holmes & Watson. If you wanted someone to be the funny sidekick to the lead in a Carry On then Butterworth was your man. Fenella Fielding vamps it up as Valaria Watt and Kenny Williams is his usual unrestrained self as the mysterious Dr Watt. He has another memorable much quoted line ("Frying tonight!") near the end. Charles Hawtrey doesn't have an awful lot to do here but Jim Dale, Joan Sims, and Bernard Bresslaw all have their moments. Look out for another Jon Pertwee cameo too.

This specific Carry On era was very into the pastiche of particular film genres and historical periods and Carry On Screaming is a great example, falling not too far behind Carry On Cleo in the pantheon of Carry On's period adventures. It's no wonder that Carry On Screaming is still a regular staple on television so many years it was produced.

(687) Two Evil Eyes is a two story horror film based on spooky tales by Edgar Allan Poe where George Romero directed one segment and Dario Argento directed the other. This project was supposed to offer four tales from the Poe catalogue and also feature contributions by Wes Craven and John Carpenter. Sadly, this didn't transpire and Craven and Carpenter dropped out after ridiculous time constraints made it impossible for them to take part.

(688) Frankenstein was written by Mary Shelley when she was only eighteen years-old. Frankenstein is a pioneering work of science fiction and an enduring touchstone of horror. To this day, rarely a year goes past without a film that was inspired by Frankenstein going into production. It is hard to think of any work of fiction that has been as influential as Frankenstein was to the horror genre. The book was written in 1818 while Mary was staying a villa near Geneva close to Lord Byron. The

story was, appropriately enough, inspired by a nightmare. The story in Frankenstein is told through the letters of an explorer named Captain Robert Walton. Walton is on an exploration of the North Pole and runs into a mysterious and cultivated Swiss scientist named Victor Frankenstein. Frankenstein has discovered a way to bring life to body parts that were previously dead. He has meddled with things that shouldn't really have been meddled with at all. The end result is the creation of a monster who inspires fear but only wants to be loved and accepted. We are faced with the realisation that the real monster may not be this unfortunate creature but Victor Frankenstein himself.

Even if you've never read Frankenstein before you might feel as if you are already familiar with this story. The mad scientist, a lightning crackled gothic laboratory, villagers with pitchforks and flaming torches. However, if that's the case you will be surprised at how the original novel subverts your expectations. This book is a lot different to how one might expect it to be from watching Frankenstein movies. The story is more complex, much bigger, more nuanced, and simply a lot more surprising than any film version you might have seen. As a consequence, Frankenstein feels like a fresh and (ahem) novel experience which is completely different to what you expected. This is one of the true landmarks and cornerstones of the horror genre but also a very moving and very human story.

(689) An American Werewolf in Paris is a 'loose' 1997 sequel to the classic 1981 John Landis horror film An American Werewolf in London. The film was directed by Anthony Waller (who also had a hand in the screenplay) and had nothing to do with John Landis. An American Werewolf in Paris is a strangely camp and silly film with an annoying grunge rock soundtrack that will start to irritate the viewer long before the film has run its course. There seems no good reason for this film to have hijacked the 'An American Werewolf in...' name and it should have just been put as a stand alone werewolf movie. An American Werewolf in Paris bombed and barely made back its production costs so the decision to position this

as a vague sequel made no difference to the commercial appeal of the film.

(690) Cube is a Canadian science fiction horror film directed and co-written by Vincenzo Natali. The film seems heavily inspired by the classic Twilight Zone episode Five Characters in Search of an Exit. Five people wake up and find themselves trapped in an elaborate steel maze full of cube shaped rooms. As they try to move through the hatches they realise that some of the rooms are equipped with deadly booby traps. The explanation for the Cube is vague in the extreme and the film rather uses this as a sick joke. Faceless bureaucracy gone mad. The idea that there might be no one in particular behind the torment, just an indifferent quango or accounting error, is quite chilling though. In a way that's more scary than some masked maniac being behind it all.

(691) Harry Dean Stanton was supposed to play Lloyd the bartender in The Shining but had to pull out because of his role in Alien.

(692) The huge success of the found footage film The Blair Witch Project saw Artisan Entertainment quickly press ahead with a sequel. Daniel Myrick and Eduardo Sánchez, who directed the first film, had little to do with this despite their producer credits. Joe Berlinger co-wrote and directed this sequel and took the film in a different direction than the original. Blair Witch 2 is not a found footage film - although it does incorporate documentary/video camera footage at times to evoke memories of this genre. Blair Witch 2 made a profit but received merciless reviews (in contrast to the much praised first film). With the passage of time, Blair Witch 2 has now suffered the traditional fate of underwhelming sequels to famous films. It has become practically invisible to the point where most people have probably forgotten it was even made in the first place.

(693) Triangle is a 2009 psychological horror thriller film written and directed by Christopher Smith. The film stars

Melissa George as Jess, a woman with an autistic son who goes on a boating trip with some friends. When the boat sinks they end up taking refuge on an ocean liner that seems to have been abandoned. But Jess has a powerful sense of deja vu. She feels as if she's been on this ship before. This horror tinged take on the recurring time loop is compelling and well played by the cast. It's a film that deserves a wider audience.

(694) 2011's The Thing was directed by Matthijs van Heijningen Jr. This is a prequel/remake of John Carpenter's classic film and ultimately proves to be unnecessary. Seems strange that it had the same title too given that it's a prequel. You'd think they would have called it something else. If you ever wondered what exactly happened at the doomed Norwegian camp in Carpenter's film, well, this 2011 version of The Thing attempts to answer that for you. It won't come as a huge surprise to learn that it involved the shapeshifting alien creature and lots of screaming. Once the characters start turning into CGI aliens at the drop of a hat the film starts to lose its way. A popular criticism of this film is that the 'thing' is used far too much, to the point where it has no mystique or scare factor. The creature was terrifying in the original because it stayed hidden so much. You genuinely had no idea if the man next to you was the alien or not. In this prequel, you end up with ridiculous scenes of the CGI thing chasing people down corridors like a monster out of a Roger Corman film.

(695) David Twohy wrote a rejected screenplay for Alien 3 set on a prison space station. The prison aspect stayed in the finished film.

(696) Ghost Stories was written and directed by Andy Nyman and Jeremy Dyson and based on their 2010 stage play of the same name. If you like anthology horror films you should enjoy this on the whole and the cast is very good. It's one of the better British horror films in recent memory and worth seeking out.

(697) Phase IV was directed by Saul Bass - best known for

designing title sequences for classic films like Psycho. Phase IV is a truly strange film but a very unique experience. The film is set in the desert where a couple of scientists (played by Nigel Davenport and Michael Murphy) living in a sealed bio dome end up matching wits against a species of ants which has gained super intelligence. The film is every bit as weird as that synopsis makes it sound but novel for a number of reasons. For one the ants are normal sized. These ants are not lumbering monsters like something out of 1950s science fiction but crafty little critters who - by the end of the film - have gained intelligence way beyond that of man. Welcome to our new insect overlords. Phase IV is not for all tastes but a very singular and trippy experience all the same. Make sure you don't miss out on watching that amazing full deleted ending.

(698) Halloween: The Curse of Michael Myers was directed by Joe Chappelle. The production of this film was an absolute bun fight by all accounts with the director and producer rewriting chunks of the screenplay and bickering with the studio. The writer Daniel Farrands hated the film because it deviated from his screenplay too much. Reshoots were ordered when a test screening panned the film. A 'producer's cut' of the film was released on DVD years later and seems to be held in slightly higher regard. The biggest problem the franchise had at this point was explaining who the 'man in black' was at the end of the last film. Well, he's a cult leader. Runes. Cults. Ancient druids. Michael is immortal and indestructible because he has been given the curse of Thorn. Isn't it scarier to just have Michael as an unexplained enigmatic evil force of nature?

(699) Dr Phibes Rises Again, the sequel to The Abominable Dr Phibes, saw Robert Fuest return to direct. This time, Phibes returns and sets off for Egypt to search for a river of eternal life. Darius Biederbeck (Robert Quarry), who has been prolonging his life with an elixir, is also after the same goal and sets off with his team. As you may imagine, with Dr Phibes at large, Biederbeck's team are going to meet some very

untimely and elaborate deaths. Dr Phibes Rises Again is essentially more of the same and - happily - that's exactly what we want. This is a sequel easily on a par with the original. Vincent Price once again rules as the completely mad Phibes and Price, in his ghoulish white face make-up, gives (if possible) an even more entertainingly bonkers performance than he did in the first film. The deaths are once again amusingly inventive with scorpions, sandblasting, and someone crushed by a giant screw-press.

(700) It! The Terror from Beyond Space was directed by Edward L Cahn. The film is based on AE Van Vogt's Voyage of the Space Beagle. It! The Terror from Beyond Space, its source text, and Mario Bava's Planet of the Vampires were the key influences for Ridley Scott's Alien. The premise of the film is simple. A spaceship picks up Colonel Edward Carruthers (Marshall Thompson), the marooned lone survivor of a mission to Mars. The nine men that Carruthers were with are dead and he's presumed guilty of murder. Carruthers maintains that some sort of creature was the culprit and that he's innocent. On the way back to Earth for the court martial of Carruthers, it transpires that the creature was real and has stowed away on the ship. Everyone is now in very great danger.

(701) Clu Gulager was only cast in Return of the Living Dead on the first day of shooting.

(702) Doom is a 2005 science fiction action horror film directed by Andrzej Bartkowiak. It is based on the legendary FPS video game series. The game, as everyone will know, has you as a space marine fighting your way through demonic monsters who seem to have been literally raised from Hell. If you are a fan of Doom you'll struggle to see much in the film that reminds you of the game - aside from a fun first person perspective sequence. This film version of Doom is basically someone riffing on James Cameron's Aliens yet again. In the film version of Doom, The Rock and Karl Urban play the leaders of a marine squad answering a distress signal from a

research base on Mars. Once there they find that the humans have been infected by something and seem to be turning into dangerous creatures. Or something like that.

Doom is very uninspired for a film of this type and doesn't have the fantastic atmosphere of the game. Disappointingly, the demonic imagery is absent and the huge base levels of the game are replaced here by a series of dimly lit corridors, stairways, and sewers. It looks at times as if they shot most of this film in one small corridor! The action in Doom is ho-hum and the film is never very frightening. The game had a nice mixture of sci-fi bases, corridors, open spaces, demonic imagery, green slime rivers, and more. This film captures none of that. If it didn't have the Doom name as the title you wouldn't even know this was supposed to be a Doom movie. Event Horizon captured more of a Doom atmosphere than this official adaptation does. A shame really as Doom surely deserved a much better film.

(703) In 2003 a new cut of Alien 3 was assembled by Charles de Lauzirika for the Alien Quadrilogy DVD. The purpose of this special edition was to show (as far as possible) what David Fincher had been trying to do and show us what had been lost in an editing room. The special edition of Alien 3 adds a whopping 30 minutes to the running time, adding new scenes and discarding some footage from the theatrical cut. Fincher declined to participate but apparently did give his blessing. Does the assembly cut make Alien 3 a better film? Yes, it certainly does. The best thing about the cut is that it allows Alien 3 to make more sense. The characters are fleshed out more and the subplot of Paul McGann's Golic worshipping the alien creature is restored. There is an extra sequence too where the characters temporarily trap the alien and Golic releases it. There are changes too to the way Ripley arrives, the animal the alien gestates in, and the ending. The alien bursting from Ripley's stomach at the end is removed (Fincher always hated this addition). The extra scene at the start where Charles Dance walks the windswept beach and discovers Ripley's oil and insect encrusted body is terrific and shows us some of the

scope that Fincher was aiming for but wasn't allowed to fulfil. The new cut of Alien 3 certainly improves the film but it remains a divisive entry in the series.

(704) The surveillance camera footage in Saw was added to the first film when director James Wan realised he didn't have enough footage for a feature length film.

(705) It is said that as part of his contract on Candyman, Tony todd had a stipulation where he was paid $1,000 for each time he endured a bee sting.

(706) Charlize Theron was originally going to play Elizabeth Shaw in Prometheus but she was unavailable because of the long production of Mad Max: Fury Road. When she was free again she joined Prometheus in the lesser role of Vickers.

(707) The Invisible Man is a 1933 Pre-Code science fiction horror film based on HG Wells' science fiction novel. The film was directed by James Whale. This is a very entertaining and enjoyable film that is powered by a fantastic performance by Claude Rains as Griffin. He genuinely seems to be having the time of his life playing a villain and scaring all the other characters witless. The invisible scenes were apparently done with wires and a black velvet suit that meshed with a background.

(708) The Evil Dead was based on a 1978 Sam Raimi short film called Within the Woods.

(709) At one point during production of the superior ghost chiller The Others, Nicole Kidman quit the film because she found the subject matter too stressful. She was however persuaded to return and finish the picture.

(710) The extras who played the zombies in the original Night of the Living Dead were paid $1 and given a free t-shirt.

(711) Michael J. Fox was allegedly considered for the role of

Jesse Walsh in A Nightmare On Elm Street.
(712) Creepshow was a rare case of George Romero working
with a generous budget. It was his most successful film and
opened at number one in the weekly box-office charts in
America.

(713) Stephen King thinks the film version of Carrie (the
original OBVIOUSLY - not the remake) is better than his book.

(714) It was something of a miracle that such a memorable
monster emerged in Predator because the film started
shooting with a completely different Predator design. Martial
arts star Jean Claude Van Damme (then largely unknown) had
been hired to play the Predator (the thinking was that his
athleticism would make the alien appear quick and
formidable) and the alien costume he was given looked like a
cross between a fly, a prawn and a dog with a big yellow eye
and spindly legs like stilts. It was atrocious and after shooting
a couple of sequences director John McTiernan sent the
Predator costume back to the studio and told them the film
would be a laughing stock if he carried on like this.

(715) ISOBAR (aka Dead Reckoning) is an unmade script from
the late eighties written by future Fight Club scribe Jim Uhls
and described as "Alien on a futuristic train". It was going to
be directed by Ridley Scott (Scott must hold some sort of
record for being attached to films that never got made) and
star Sylvester Stallone. I'd pay money to watch that. Alien on a
futuristic train with Sylvester Stallone!

(716) Donald Sutherland, later to become a star through films
like M*A*S*H, Kelly's Heroes and Don't Look Now, was an
unknown Canadian actor based in Britain at the time of the
1965 horror anthology classic Dr Terror's House of Horrors.
He had studied at the London Academy of Music and
Dramatic Art and spent a year and a half in Repertory Theatre
in Scotland. Dr Terror's House of Horrors was one of his early
roles. Sutherland got $5,400 for the film and a free ride to
work every morning with producer Max Rosenberg.

(717) A proposed but unmade Tales from the Crypt movie was Dead Easy. Dead Easy was described as a zombie romp set in New Orleans. Gilbert Adler told Fangoria magazine that the screenplay was shelved because it was too dark and didn't have the trademark Tales from the Crypt humour. There are stories - most likely apocryphal - that Dead Easy (also known as Fat Tuesday) was actually shot but then locked in a vault by Joel Silver because the black cast in the New Orleans set story were 'whitewashed' and replaced with a white cast. Silver, so the story goes, thought they would be slated for racism if they ever released the film. The notion of Dead Easy as some sort of horror version of The Day the Clown Cried can probably be taken with a pinch of salt.

(718) David Goyer wrote the character of Whistler in Blade with Patrick McGoohan in mind.

(719) Critters 4 is a 1992 science fiction comedy horror film directed by Rupert Harvey. The Critters franchise was sort of like a vague bargain basement rip-off of Gremlins - the Critters being furry little aliens with fanged teeth who roll around in a ball and cause all manner of bloodthirsty mischief. This fourth entry (like many other long running horror franchises) tries to freshen things up by moving the action into space and going for more of a sci-fi feel. The dimwitted bounty hunter Charlie McFadden (Don Keith Opper) - the lead character of this franchise - is, as usual, battling the Critters but winds up being transported to the year 2045 where the Critters soon abound on a spaceship. So, basically, this is the Critters franchise riffing on Alien - albeit in tongue in cheek fashion (the Critters films are not exactly subtle with humour). Critters 4 is watchable enough if you like low-budget eighties/nineties horror sci-fi and although the designs and sets are no great shakes you do get a surprisingly decent cast given the modest nature of the film. Angela Bassett and Brad Dourif (both of whom are probably far too good for this nonsense) plus Twin Peaks star Eric Da Re. The voice of the ship's computer is supplied by Hammer and James Bond star Martine Beswick.

(720) Dino De Laurentiis boasted that his 1976 King Kong remake would have incredible special effects and that Kong would be brought to life by a state of the art robotic model. This huge mechanical Kong was built at a cost of well over one million dollars but proved to be so useless it only features in the actual film for 15 seconds! The Kong in the finished film is a just a man in a monkey suit - which is exactly what they boasted they wouldn't do.

(721) Evil Dead 2 is more or less a remake but perhaps even more of a tour de force from director Sam Raimi, a sort of horror version of The Three Stooges with Bruce Campbell as The Three Stooges waging an increasingly bloody and comical battle against haunted inanimate objects, demons and all manner of spooky things.

(722) A fairly well received television movie about the serial killer John Wayne Gacy called To Catch a Killer was made in 1992. It starred the always reliable Brian Dennehy as Gacy. Gacy was killed by lethal injection a few years after the film. Gacy is one of the most evil serial killers in the history of the United States (and given the competition that's really saying something). Gacy murdered 33 teenage boys and young men between 1972 and 1978. John Wayne Gacy's access to victims was provided by his construction business. He was constantly in contact with teenagers and young men looking for some temporary work. One of John Wayne Gacy's methods of getting his victims handcuffed was to pretend he was demonstrating a magic trick. He would escape from the handcuffs himself and then challenge the victim to do the same. Gacy would usually try and get his victims a bit drunk for this game. By the time they realised it was not a game and that Gacy was dangerous it was all too late. They were already helpless. John Wayne Gacy weighed 230 pounds. He was a big man who would have been difficult to fight off - especially if one was restrained.

Gacy stuffed the bodies of most of his victims in the

crawlspace of his home. When his wife asked about the smell he told her it was mice. Gacy used his experience as a mortician's assistant to block the cavities of his victims with rags and underwear. This prevented too much leakage after death. John Wayne Gacy would sometimes contact the police and report one of the men he had killed as missing. This was a tactic designed to make him seem trustworthy and throw the police off his scent. Many of John Wayne Gacy's victims were found to have rope tied around their neck. It was an exceptionally complex and time consuming task to identify all of the victims. Sadly, to this day, there are still victims of Gacy yet to be identified.

Gacy was sentenced to death on twelve counts of murder and spent fourteen years on Death Row before he was executed in 1994. In 2003 there was another film about this killer simply entitled Gacy. Mark Holton played Gacy in this straight to DVD film. It got terrible reviews. A third Gacy film is 2010's Dear Mr Gacy. This film is based on a memoir by Jason Moss. Moss corresponded with Gacy when Gacy was in prison in an attempt to learn more about serial killers. He even personally met Gacy in prison (and found Gacy to be a powerful and manipulative sociopath). Gacy famously dressed up as a clown to entertain the local children. John Wayne Gacy actually had two different personas when he dressed up as a clown. Sometimes he was Pogo the Clown and sometimes he was Patches the Clown. These two 'characters' had their own costume. It comes as no great surprise then to learn that Gacy would become forever known as The Clown Killer. After his death, John Wayne Gacy's Pogo the Clown costume was put on display at the Alcatraz East crime museum.

(723) Gunnar Hansen did not play Leatherface in The Texas Chainsaw Massacre 2 because he felt his proposed salary was too low.

(724) Doodles Weaver, who plays a fisherman in Hitchcock's The Birds, was the uncle of Sigourney Weaver.

(725) Selena Gomez was considered for the part played by Emma Roberts in Scream 4.

(726) The Last Broadcast, a 1998 found footage film by Stefan Avalos and Lance Weiler, is believed by many to have influenced Blair Witch but the makers of Blair denied this.

(727) One thing that highlights Creepshow 2's modest budget are the framing sequences featuring some truly awful animation of Billy and the Creepshow Creep.

(728) Some of the corpses hanging around in the basement in the film Dog Soldiers were originally created for and used in Event Horizon.

(729) Alien 2: On Earth (also known as Alien Terror and 'Strangers') is a 1980 science fiction horror film written and directed by Ciro Ippolito. This low-budget Italian exploitation film had the chutzpah to call itself Alien 2 and received a lawsuit from 20th Century Fox as a consequence. Alien 2: On Earth was allowed to keep its title though because the 'Alien' name had already been used in a book as the title decades ago. 20th Century Fox could hardly claim they had invented the term. Alien 2: On Earth is something of a snorefest although it does have a couple of enjoyably nasty gore scenes with old school special effects. The plot, such as it is, makes little sense and mostly revolves around caving. A space expedition (which we learn of at the start of the film) is due back and, to cut to the chase, little snake like aliens seem to be lurking in the caves where the main characters are trying to enjoy a spot of spelunking. As you might imagine, these aliens eventually cause some bloodthirsty carnage when our unsuspecting spelunkers stumble across them.

Alien 2: On Earth is a lot duller than it sounds (if you want a horror film about caving watch The Descent instead) and has only vague similarities to Alien - those being the constrictive location and the fact that the alien creatures apparently gestate in human hosts. For those who do manage to stick it out though you will get a rather gruesome 'faceburster' sequence and a decapitation - all done with old fashioned make-up effects. The film is worth watching for the gloopy gore effects but that aside it doesn't have a huge amount going for it despite the fact that underground caves usually make an interesting location for horror movies.

(730) Hammer and Amicus maestro Elisabeth Lutyens was the first woman to compose the score for a horror film.

(731) The 'Leprechaun' horror franchise was one of the more durable in the field despite its relative obscurity. The fourth entry in 1996 took a detour into Alien territory with Leprechaun 4: In Space. The plot, such as it is, has Warwick Davis as the title character - a little demonic Irish Leprechaun who kills people in comical fashion. Anyway, the Leprechaun ends up on a ship full of space marines (who think they've killed him but naturally haven't in reality) in the future and, as you would imagine, the body count soon starts to pile up. If you've never seen a Leprechaun film you have no particular reason to change that but this fourth entry does have a bizarre novelty if nothing else by dint of placing this rather silly horror villain in an Alien type backdrop (albeit a very low-budget one). The humour in this film (and the series as a whole one would imagine) is rather grating but this is surreal enough to qualify as a late night oddity for those with nothing better to do. The director was Ozploitation filmmaker Brian Trenchard-Smith of BMX Bandits and Turkey Shoot.

(732) Originally Stripe and Gizmo in Gremlins were the same character. It was changed so that there was at least one sympathetic gremlin.

(733) Scream was originally a screenplay by Kevin Williamson called Scary Movie.

(734) John Hurt was one of the top choices for the part of Hannibal Lecter in Silence of the Lambs but illness prevented this from happening.

(735) For the scene in The Thing in which Dr. Copper (Richard Dysart) has his arms severed, a double amputee stand-in was used wearing a Richard Dysart mask.

(736) Shaun's cricket bat in Shaun of the Dead was a soft padded fake so that Simon Pegg could actually whack zombie extras.

(737) The Ghostface mask in Wes Craven's Scream is based on the The Scream by Edvard Munch.

(738) The post-apocalyptic feel of Escape from New York was aided by shooting the film in parts of St Louis which were ravaged by fires in the seventies.

(739) Richard Matheson of I Am Legend and The Twilight Zone fame was the original writer of Jaws 3. Matheson claims his story was pretty good and with a decent director it could have been an excellent film. Sadly though, Matheson's story was constantly changed and rewritten. Matheson was very bitter about the whole thing. He felt the finished film was murky looking and the 3-D was pointless. He also thought the director Joe Alves was useless

(740) Arnold Schwarzenegger was originally put up for the role of Kyle Reese in The Terminator. James Cameron thought it was a terrible suggestion but it occurred to him that Schwarzenegger would make an excellent Terminator instead.

(741) The 2007 portmanteau horror film Trick 'r' Treat written and directed by Michael Dougherty sat on the shelf for two years and never even got a theatrical release but is now enjoying a deserved second wind as a cult favourite and Halloween staple.

(742) The ending of Army of Darkness was deemed too downbeat by the studio so Sam Raimi had to shoot a new one. You can see the original ending on the director's cut. Raimi

said he likes the fact that two endings exist because it's Ash in two different alternate realities.

(743) Sissy Spacek did not mix with the cast on the set of Carrie as she wanted to method act being an outsider.

(744) Sandra Bullock was second choice for the part played by Virginia Madsen in Candyman.

(745) David Fincher was in line to direct Blade at an early stage of its development.

(746) Lead actor James Brolin took a share of the profits rather than a salary on The Amityville Horror. This gamble paid off when The Amityville Horror became a blockbuster.

(747) Believe it or not, before Schwarzenegger was cast, the studio actually proposed OJ Simpson as the Terminator.

(748) George Romero's 1972 film Season of the Witch began shooting as Jack's Wife, a feminist drama about a trapped housewife who dreams of something exciting happening to her. When Romero's funding suddenly proved problematic the director had to shoot the film for only half the budget that had been originally estimated. He finished the film but the lack of money created havoc with his original vision for the picture and many scenes were either scrapped altogether or shortened. A distributor who picked up the film was so dismayed by this talky low-budget drama's obvious lack of commercial appeal he shamelessly changed the title to Hungry Wives and tried to market it as a sex film - which it most certainly wasn't.

(749) When the Hannibal script was behind schedule producer Dino De Laurentiis sent his personal pasta chef to cook for writer Thomas Harris to spur him on!

(750) The strangest cast member in Dr Terror's House of Horrors is surely Alan "Fluff" Freeman. The disc jockey and

Top of the Pops presenter played Bill Rogers in the "killer plant" segment of the film. Freeman was tentatively exploring an acting career at the time but his wooden performance in Dr Terror's House of Horrors seemed to put an end to this ambition.

(751) The sequence where the demonic car restores itself in John Carpenter's Christine was done by special effects expert Roy Arbogast. Metal was essentially sucked down vents and then the process was reversed on film to get the required effect. The sequence is amusingly framed to be rather like a striptease.

(752) A young Greg Nicotero was a make-up artist on George Romero's Day of the Dead under Tom Savini. Nicotero is now special effects chief and frequent director on The Walking Dead. Nicotero also plays Pvt. Johnson, one of the soldiers, in the film.

(753) The Blair Witch Project was shot in just eight days. The three cast members shot everything and were reacting to random scares thrown at them by the directors.

(754) It was the success of the first Blade film that gave Hollywood renewed confidence in superhero films after Batman & Robin and 'Steel' had met a hostile critical reception.

(755) Medieval England in Sam Raimi's Army of Darkness is quite obviously California!

(756) Walter Hill and David Giler liked Dan O'Bannon's premise for Alien but thought his screenplay was terrible so they rewrote it. One major change by Giler and Hill was creating the android Ash played by Ian Holm.

(757) The most iconic thing about Westworld is undoubtedly the late Yul Brynner's remorseless and stoic black/grey clad robot gunslinger - who is essentially Arnie in The Terminator

years before that film was devised. John Carpenter said that Michael Myers, his unstoppable bogeyman killer from Halloween, was partly inspired by Yul Brynner's malfunctioning robot.

(758) John Carpenter considers The Thing part of his Apocalypse Trilogy. The other two films in that trilogy are Prince of Darkness and In the Mouth of Madness.

(759) Aileen Wuornos is arguably the most famous female serial killer - mostly thanks to a film and documentary which were made about her crimes. Charlize Theron won an Oscar for portraying Aileen Wuornos in the 2003 film Monster. Wuornos killed seven men in total from 1989 to 1990. She had a tough start in life and an abusive upbringing at the hands of a strict grandfather. Wuornos was a surprisingly beautiful child but a tough life obviously extracted a cruel toll on her looks in the end. She was homeless at fifteen and sold her body to survive. Tired of the cold, she eventually hitchhiked to Florida and married a rich man. The marriage only lasted days. He put a restraining order on her because Wournos would beat him up. Aileen Wuornos was a notoriously volatile person with an unpredictable (and rather frightening) temper.

After her marriage collapsed, Aileen Wuornos worked as a prostitute and, in desperate need of money, turned to murder. She picked up her victims on the I-75 highway. She would always target middle-aged men in nice cars. Once she was picked up, Wuornos would start to undress in the car and ask the driver to pull over somewhere secluded. Then she would get out of the car and shoot them before stealing their wallets. Aileen Wuornos would often shoot her victims multiple times. Her alleged motivation for the murders was that she wanted to support her girlfriend and lover Ty. One might argue that a hatred of men was rather evident too. Psychologist Marissa Harrison concluded from her study that female serial killers were mostly motivated by material gain whereas male serial killers were mostly motivated by sexual urges. Aileen Wuornos was clearly motivated by her desperate desire to get quick money. Wuornos never really did much to hide the bodies of the victims. They were found fairly quickly and easily. A few men had a lucky escape from Aileen Wuornos. One man actually saw the gun in her purse and managed to drive away wile she was outside the vehicle. Aileen Wuornos was captured when the police finally managed to get an accurate artists impression of the killer who was shooting these motorists. Once this sketch was circulated, they soon had a lot of calls telling them the illustration looked a lot like Aileen Wuornos - an angry and violent local woman who seemed to spend most of her spare time drinking beer in biker bars. Wuornos was taken into custody and the police discovered that she had sold the belongings (like wristwatches and jewelry) of the victims in local pawn shops. Any money they had she of course kept for herself.

Aileen Wuornos claimed that she had killed the men in self-defence because they all tried to rape her. This was seen as a weak and highly improbable defence. It appeared very unlikely that seven different men all tried to rape her at different times on the exact same stretch of highway. One of the victims was selling Bibles and another was a former police chief. They were ordinary people with no criminal history. The fact that Wuornos had not reported a single one of these incidents and always tried to hide the bodies also made her rape defence seem less than plausible. Aileen Wuornos eventually pleaded guilty to five murders because she wanted the death penalty. She was tired of prison and court hearings. Aileen Wuornos felt betrayed and alone in the end. Even her beloved girlfriend Ty secretly taped their phone conversations and testified against her. Wuornos became a born again Christian after her conviction. She always got offended when someone called her a serial killer. Wuornos claimed she was not a serial killer because she never tortured or mutilated her victims. While this was true she did shoot dead several innocent men! Aileen Wuornos was executed in 2002. Wuornos declined a last meal before her execution and simply asked for black coffee. For $15 on crime collectible websites you can buy a photograph of Aileen Wuornos posing with a friend before her execution. She looks surprisingly happy in the photo considering the circumstances in which it was taken. Aileen Wuornos was a twist on the common serial killer situation in that she was a prostitute but a killer rather than a victim. She said she wasn't evil but just had a consuming hatred for the human race.

(760) Isaac Hayes, Geoffrey Holder, Carl Weathers, Ernie Hudson and Bernie Casey were considered for the part of Childs in The Thing.

(761) Jason X is a 2001 science fiction horror film directed by James Isaac. It is the tenth installment in the Friday the 13th film series. This film sends the hockey mask wearing maniac Jason Voorhees into the future after he is placed in stasis and unwittingly thawed out in the year 2455 after being taken aboard a spaceship. Well, as you might imagine, Jason is soon up to his old tricks and killing off the crew as carnage abounds. Jason X got terrible reviews but it is a fun film if you approach it in the right frame of mind and Lisa Ryder's android KM-14 is almost worth the price of admission alone. The special effects are serviceable and you get one or two inventive kills. None of this is to be taken seriously but it's a novelty if nothing else to see Jason aboard a spaceship in the future killing off the crew like Giger's Alien. There's a jokey tone to proceedings so none of the film is very scary but it does pass the time if you park your brain in neutral and accept Jason X for what it is. Look out by the way for a cameo near the start by David Cronenberg.

(762) The gas station sign in The Texas Chainsaw Massacre seems to imply the Sawyers are not the Sawyers but the Slaughters.

(763) Lecter's cell in The Silence of the Lambs is designed to be like a journey down to hell.

(764) The mask in Wes Craven's Scream was developed for Halloween in 1991 by Fun World and was originally given the name The Peanut-Eyed Ghost.

(765) Note how cars are still on the bridge when the zombies are supposed to be taking over New York at the end of Zombi 2. This is because the production didn't have enough money to close off the bridge to traffic.

(766) John Landis was offered the chance to direct The Thing before the job was given to John Carpenter.

(767) Parasite is a 1982 film directed by Charles Band (a cultish low-budget filmmaker responsible for pictures like Trancers). This film makes an earnest if doomed attempt to evoke (then recent hits) Alien and Mad Max. Parasite is set in the near future in the aftermath of nuclear devastation. There is no government anymore and a sinister group known as Merchants run the United States - now a desolate place where food is scarce. The parasite action is far too rationed in the film although you do get a stomach burster sequence that homages Alien and there's quite an enjoyable scene where an annoying landlady runs into the parasite (with predictably dire consequences for her). This film is most famous now for an early role by Demi Moore. You'd be hard pressed to predict that Demi Moore would become a big star on the strength of this film.

(768) The killer's robe in Wes Craven's Scream was initially going to be white but was switched to black to avoid any similarity to Ku Klux Klan attire.

(769) The supermarket in Shaun of the Dead is called Landis in tribute to John Landis.

(770) Peter Cushing and Michael York were offered the role of Sgt Howie in The Wicker Man but both were unavailable.

(771) The western set for the original Westworld movie was used in Blazing Saddles.

(772) Jeremy Licht, who plays the all powerful little boy in Joe

Dante's remake of It's A Good Life for Twilight Zone: The Movie, drifted out of acting and became a registered investment advisor.

(773) Special effects wiz Rob Bottin used bubblegum for some of the head stretching effects in John Carpenter's The Thing.

(774) The Texas Chainsaw Massacre 2 was originally going to be called Beyond the Valley Of The Texas Chainsaw Massacre.

(775) Jonathan Demme is said to have wanted Sean Connery to play Hannibal Lecter in Silence of the Lambs but Connery found the material too distasteful.

(776) The frosty maze at the end of The Shining is made of crushed Styrofoam and salt.

(777) There are a number of elaborate conspiracy theories about The Shining. One is that Kubrick apparently leaves a trail of clues in the film that serve as a confession that he helped NASA fake the moon landings!

(778) The Winchester in Shaun of the Dead used to be a real pub.

(779) DeepStar Six is a 1989 film directed by Sean S Cunningham. This is another of the underwater horror films that abounded in 1989. A deep sea crew researching the possibilities of underwater colonization cause an underground cavern to collapse and run foul of a giant sea monster that looks like a large crab. And that's only the start of the trouble. Can they evade the monster and get to the surface before all of their equipment and escape pods are destroyed? Deepstar Six is a little forgotten these days but it's the least pretentious of 1989's more high profile underwater thrillers and perfectly competent for what it is (basically an undersea version of Alien). You have to wait an awful long time to see the monster though - although it does make a fine entrance into the movie by biting Police Academy's Matt McCoy in half!

(780) Molly Ringwald turned down the part of Sid in Wes Craven's Scream. Ringwald, then in her late twenties, felt she was too old to still be playing high school students.

(781) Saw was intended to be a straight to DVD release but turned out to be a highly profitable theatrical film.

(782) Predator had the second biggest opening weekend gross of any film in 1987.

(783) The Blair monster at the end of John Carpenter's The Thing was going to be stop-motion but they didn't feel it looked convincing enough.

(784) Charlie Sheen was nearly cast to play Glen in A Nightmare On Elm Street but wanted too much money.

(785) It was Stephen King who persuaded the producer Dino De Laurentiis to fund Evil Dead II. This happened when they were working on Maximum Overdrive together.

(786) Richard Dreyfuss badmouthed Jaws and told everyone it was going to be terrible. He soon changed his tune when the reviews started coming in.

(787) Gary Oldman based Verger's voice in Hannibal on Katharine Hepburn.

(788) The name of the Donald Pleasance character in Halloween is also the name of Janet Leigh's boyfriend in Psycho. Halloween star Jamie Lee Curtis was the daughter of Janet Leigh in real life.

(789) Emilio Estevez and Judd Nelson were considered for the part of Billy in Gremlins. These two would soon appear together in the cult John Hughes film The Breakfast Club.

(790) Christopher Lee is said to have got really bored of

playing Dracula in the Hammer films. One of the reasons he liked The Wicker Man so much was that he felt it was a role that might free him of his Dracula typecasting shackles. This probably explains why Lee was so annoyed when The Wicker Man was a flop (due to incompetent marketing).

(791) Contamination is a 1980 Italian horror film directed by Luigi Cozzi. The story revolves around strange green pulsating eggs which are found on a ship in New York which drifted in and was obviously failing to respond to communication. Bodies are found on the ship which look as if they have exploded from the inside (sounds familiar!) - just to deepen the mystery. The authorities who investigate the ship soon realise why there are bodies seemingly torn to shreds. It transpires that the green eggs are highly toxic to humans and if you come into contact with their residue your flesh will literally explode. Colonel Stella Holmes (Louise Marleau) and former astronaut Ian Hubbard (Ian McCulloch) must investigate what is going on and in the process will stumble into a big conspiracy. Contamination has some very big parallels to Alien with people's stomachs exploding and also the flashback scene where we see hundreds of the aliens eggs in a cave on Mars.

Early on you get the exploding bodies and think this is going to be a very gruesome exploitation film (Contamination was caught up in the 'video nasty' furore in Britain) but the gore is quite restrained - or rationed at least - from here on in. It's fun when it does arrive though. You can't help thinking it's a shame really that the film is set on Earth (presumably to save money) as the Mars flashback scene is quite well done. Luigi Cozzi did make Starcrash so a space film on a low budget wouldn't have been a new experience for him. Contamination is a typically Italian low-budget film in the way it mashes genres - becoming something of an espionage caper in a slightly dull middle section before picking up at the end when we get a cyclops monster (which is wisely not shown for too long but fun anyway). Contamination is no classic but it's watchable and in Ian McCulloch at least has a decent actor at the heart of the story and that's not something you can say about all of these eighties Alien clones.

(792) Vincent Price and the cast said they found it hard not to laugh making 1958's The Fly - such was the ludicrous (but enjoyable) plot.

(793) Potential alternative titles for The Evil Dead were The Book of the Dead, Blood Flood, and The Evil Dead Men and the Evil Dead Women.

(794) The actor, musician, and later beloved children's entertainer/presenter Roy Castle was added to Dr Terror's House of Horrors as jazz trumpeter "Biff" Bailey after Acker Bilk had to bail out due to ill health.

(795) It takes a long time for the monsters to show up in The Descent. Director Neil Marshall said he wanted claustrophobia to be the terror and then just when you think things can't get any worse...they do!

(796) The mall used in Zack Snyder's Dawn of the Dead was real but defunct and abandoned. It was demolished after shooting.

(797) The 'Crate' monster in Creepshow was known as 'Fluffy' to the crew.

(798) Drew Goddard said The Cabin in the Woods was designed as an antidote to 'torture porn' horror films where the characters act like idiots and the plots are little more than a series of sadistic comeuppances

(799) Steve McQueen took a flat modest fee rather than a profit share deal on The Blob. This was a big mistake because the film was very profitable.

(800) Alien star Veronica Cartwright, a child actress of the era, appears in Hitchcock's The Birds. She was 13 at the time.

(801) David Naughton was best known for Dr Pepper commercials before he appeared in An American Werewolf in London.

(802) Screenwriter Dan O'Bannon used the 1974 John Carpenter comedy Dark Star as the basis for Alien.

(803) The biggest difference between Aliens vs Predator: Requiem and the first Alien vs Predator film is that the nastiness factor is increased considerably. They seem to go out of their way in this one to shock at times. The start of the film has a father and son in the woods stumbling across some facehuggers and both ending up with a facehugger impaled on their face. Later on, in a disgusting scene, a pregnant woman in hospital is forcibly mouth raped by the Predator/Alien hybrid creature.

(804) Lifeforce is an adaptation of a novel called Space Vampires. The producers felt that 'Space Vampires' was too B-movie a title and so changed it to Lifeforce.

(805) The creepy commercials for Silver Shamrock in Halloween III are to the tune of London Bridge is Falling Down.

(806) Michael Biehn was furious when he found out that Hicks was being killed off offscreen in Alien 3 and that they were using his image without his permission. Biehn made the studio pay a fee to use his likeness.

(807) The 1986 film Henry: Portrait of a Serial Killer was based on Ottiss Toole and Henry Lee Lucas. Ottis Toole was a Florida born serial killer who confessed to over a hundred murders (he was officially convicted of six murders at his trial but DNA evidence suggested this was merely the tip of the iceberg). He is believed to have gone on a killing spree with Henry Lee Lucas. Toole had a very low IQ and his mother was said to be crazy and involved in occult rituals. Though

sentenced to death, the execution was never carried out and Toole died in prison in 1996 at the age of 49.

(808) Tobey Maguire was the original choice to play the human lead in Rise of the Planet of the Apes. However, when Maguire started suggesting changes to the script they replaced him with - somewhat ironically - his Spider-Man co-star James Franco.

(809) One of the obvious problems people have with found footage films is that it often seems implausible that you would constantly keep filming in the midst of a terrifying life or death situation!

(810) The final POV shot in The Evil Dead where the demonic force races at Ash through the woods was done by mounting a camera on front of a motorbike.

(811) Because David calls Prince Charles' sexuality into question in An American werewolf in London, a disclaimer was added to the credits which read "Lycanthrope films limited wishes to extend its heartfelt congratulations to Lady Diana Spencer and His Royal Highness the Prince of Wales on the occasion of their marriage - July 29th 1981".

(812) A Jason vs Leatherface horror comic book depicted Jason Vorheees and Leatherface meeting and doing battle.

(813) Sigourney Weaver's fee for Alien Resurrection was larger than the production budget for the first Alien picture.

(814) When Dinosaurs Ruled the Earth is a 1970 film and another in Hammer's line of prehistoric 'ahistorical' epics where supermodel women in fur lined bikinis dodge dinosaurs.

This was based on an outline by JG Ballard and earned an Oscar nomination for its special effects.

(815) Sadly, two of the proposed stories in Creepshow 2 were not filmed due to budgetary constraints and so Creepshow 2 only has three segments as opposed to five. Cat from Hell was later used for Tales from the Darkside: The Movie. The other jettisoned story, Pinfall, was going to be about a bowling team who resort to murder and meet a most gruesome EC Comics style end at the bowling alley.

(816) Comedians Jay Leno and Gary Shandling read for the part of Palmer in John Carpenter's The Thing.

(817) Tisa Farrow, one of the stars of Zombi 2, is the sister of Mia Farrow. She only made two more films after this before retiring from acting.

(818) Curse of Frankenstein was the first film to show blood in glorious colour.

(819) Dead Ringers is a 1988 psychological horror/drama directed by David Cronenberg and based on Bari Wood and Jack Geasland's book Twins - which was to have been the name of the film too until a certain Arnold Schwarzenegger/Danny DeVito high concept but low on laughs comedy of the same year got there first. In a departure from Cronenberg's (at the time) more usual visceral fare, Dead Ringers is very restrained and spare and revolves around successful, accomplished and somewhat odd twin gynaecologists Beverly and Elliot Mantle - both played by Jeremy Irons in a brilliant dual performance.

(820) The derivative (and on the face of it apparently ludicrous) premise and a very troubled production had many (including STARBURST magazine in particular) predicting that Predator was a disaster in the making. They turned out to be completely wrong.

(821) Night of the Creeps is a cult 1986 low-budget sci-fi horror film written and directed by Fred Dekker. Night of the Creeps throws in every B-film horror/science fiction reference

imaginable and like many eighties horror films has its tongue planted in cheek, riffing as it does on 1950s paranoia sci-fi and the conventions of the eighties college campus comedy film. It's like Night of the Living Dead, Dawn of the Dead, It Came from Outer Space and Invasion of the Body Snatchers all blended together with a John Hughes film and Revenge of the Nerds.

(822) Nightmares is a largely forgotten four story horror anthology released in 1983 and directed by Joseph Sargent. Sargent directed The Taking of Pelham One, Two Three and was a solid television director but he is most famous for Jaws: The Revenge and probably has the Razzies to prove it. Three of the segments here were produced for an anthology television series called Darkroom but Universal decided to film a fourth segment and shunt them all into this theatrical feature instead. It was probably an attempt to latch onto the success of George Romero's Creepshow the previous year but Nightmares didn't do terribly well and is only really remembered today for the third story (The Bishop of Battle) where a young Emilio Estevez obsessively attempts to reach the mythical thirteenth level of a weird computer arcade game.

(823) 1981 was the year of the werewolf film. There was An American Werewolf in London, The Howling, and a lesser known but interesting cult lupine thriller called Wolfen which was directed by Michael Wadleigh and based on a novel by Whitley Strieber. This is a more introspective mystical take on the genre and also fuses a gritty police thriller with lycanthropic horror to quite good effect.

(824) There are deaths aplenty in John Carpenter's Halloween but it isn't a particularly nasty or graphic film and places more emphasis on suspense than blood.

(825) Kurt Russell was genuinely surprised by the force of the dynamite blast near the end of The Thing when he throws it at the creature.

(826) Steven Spielberg said he briefly considered directing Jaws 2 but that he'd had such a terrible time on the first film that he couldn't face going out to sea again. Joe Alves, the production designer, second unit director, and eventual director (with Jaws 3), says that when John D Brown was fired they approached Spielberg to come back but Spielberg wanted one million dollars and a big profit share deal so the studio decided not to bother in their pursuit of him anymore.

(827) The 1996 film The Island of Dr Moreau was a dream project for Richard Stanley and his mystical and epic script was enough to get him the job of directing it. However, Stanley's dream job turned into a nightmare when he was sacked and replaced after just four days of shooting! Stanley sneaked back onto the set as one of Moreau's animal hybrid extras after he was sacked to see how things were going! Fairuza Balk, who plays the cat girl in the film, disappeared in protest after Stanley was sacked and had to be forced to come back to the production.

(828) A really sad note of Jaws: The Revenge is that Judith Barsi, who plays Mike Brody's daughter, tragically died at only 10 years of age due to homicide the following year. She was a child actress who appeared in commercials and on television and was famous for starring in films such as The Land Before Time, and All Dogs Go to Heaven. She suffered physical and mental abuse from her father who ended up killing both Judith and her mother Maria before shooting himself. Judith's parents were Hungarian immigrants fleeing communism in their country.

(829) Anthony Shaffer wrote a sequel to The Wicker Man where Edward Woodward's character was rescued from the burning wicker man. This sequel never got made.

(830) The Predator in Aliens v Predator: Requiem was known as Wolf to the crew because - like Harvey Keitel in Pulp Fiction - he's on a mission to mask evidence and clean up a mess.

(831) The effect of Yul Brynner's android gunslinger having acid thrown in his face in Westworld was achieved with alka-seltzer.

(832) In the early nineties Roland Emmerich was hired to direct an Alien v Predator film but it never happened in the end.

(833) Steven Spielberg earned an incredible $250 million from his profit share deal on Jurassic Park.

(834) Over the course of Predator, you can see Schwarzenegger's character Dutch start to look a bit gaunt. This is because Schwarzenegger got ill eating the local Mexican food and so stopped eating (as much as he could). He did one scene with an IV bottle in his arm.

(835) Robert A Heinlein's novel Starship Troopers was a major influence on Aliens.

(836) Peter Benchley, author of the book Jaws is based on, said he regretted depicting Great White Sharks as heartless killers. He later became an ocean conservationist.

(837) Predator 2 was the first film to be given the newly instituted NC-17 rating in the United States.

(838) The Goblin rock soundtrack in Dawn of the Dead was more prominent at first but George Romero thought the film would be even more atmospheric with 'muzak' spliced in.

(839) Gillian Anderson was considered for the part of Clarice Starling in Hannibal before it went to Julianne Moore. Anderson would later appear in the Hannibal TV series.

(840) The most bizarre Alien 3 treatment to surface was credited to Eric Red, the writer of The Hitcher and Near Dark. It involved a rural Kansas like colony in outer space where the military was creating alien/farm animal hybrids!

(841) John Landis came up with the idea for An American Werewolf in London while he was an extra on the film Kelly's Heroes.

(842) Michel Gothard was originally cast as Colonel Caine in Lifeforce but then switched to Dr Leonard Bukovsky. Gothard was said to be upset that he was demoted to a more secondary role.

(843) William Gibson's early Alien 3 script featuring the aliens as a sort of cold war weapon being fought over by rival corporations was rejected.

(844) George Romero's 1985 film Day of the Dead was originally intended to be an epic set on an island where some of the zombies had been brought under control and used as an army. It was supposed to feature 'helicopters flying into battle against zombies and playing Amazing Grace on the PA system' but was drastically changed when Romero refused to compromise on the rating the film would have and therefore failed to get $6.5 million required to bring his original vision to life.

(845) 1979's Screams of a Winter Night is a horror anthology directed by James L Wilson and made with student actors who were attending Northwestern State University in Natchitoches, Louisiana. The film features three stories and the framing device has some youngsters staying at a remote cabin on Lake Durand. This area is supposed to be cursed and locals tend not to go go here. A murder once took place at the cabin and a howling supernatural wind is said to batter the house. Our youngsters decide to tell spooky stories while in the cabin and we return back to them after each tale. This framing section becomes a substantial part of the film and is really quite good. One could even say that the characters spinning these stories in the windblown cabin is actually scarier than the three stories we then see in the segments. There are some interesting things to note about Screams of a Winter Night. It's

one of the first of the 'kids go to a cabin in the woods' horror movies and might well have been an influence on The Evil Dead. The last sequence in the film where the cabin is battered by a supernatural hurricane and objects are flying everywhere is pure Evil Dead.

(846) Charlton Heston and William Holden both turned down the lead role (eventually played by Gregory Peck) in The Omen. Holden did take a major role in the sequel though.

(847) There is a "Bub's Pizzas" in Shaun of the Dead. This is a reference to the 'intelligent' zombie Bub in George Romero's Day of the Dead.

(848) David Cronenberg only agreed to be in Jason X on condition that his character be killed By Jason Vorhees.

(849) Zac Effron became the last (at the time of writing) actor to play Ted Bundy in the 2019 Netflix film Extremely Wicked, Shockingly Evil, and Vile. The film is based on Elizabeth Kloepfer's book The Phantom Prince and takes its title from the closing comments of the Judge in Bundy's trial - "The court finds that both of these killings were indeed heinous, atrocious and cruel. And that they were extremely wicked, shockingly evil, vile and the product of a design to inflict a high degree of pain and utter indifference to human life." Lily Collins portrays Bundy's girlfriend Liz Kendall (Elizabeth Kloepfer) in the movie. The film is about Elizabeth Kloepfer's growing suspicion of Bundy although the story seems to lose focus and drift from this at some point. You don't get to see Bundy kill anyone in the movie but there is a very gripping sequence depicting's Bundy's escape from the courthouse library. Extremely Wicked, Shockingly Evil, and Vile has the best production values of any Ted Bundy film and a terrific cast but the general consensus is that the film (though well made) didn't really justify its existence or tell us anything we didn't already know about this already well chronicled maniac. I would imagine that most true crime buffs have read The Phantom Prince and are familiar with the story of Ted Bundy

and so you can't help feeling that Extremely Wicked, Shockingly Evil, and Vile won't tell anyone anything they didn't already know. The trial scenes near the end are very good though - in no small way thanks to John Malkovich as Judge Edward Cowart. The verbal jousting between Bundy and Cowart is very compelling in the movie.

(850) Altered States is a 1980 science fiction horror film by Ken Russell based on a novel by Paddy Chayefsky. The story is based on real life experiments by physician, neuroscientist, psychoanalyst, psychonaut, and philosopher Dr John Cunningham Lilly. Lilly invented the sensory deprivation tank. He saw the sensory deprivation tank as a means to explore the nature of human consciousness and used psychedelic drugs in his experiments. In the film, William Hurt plays a university professor who experiments with other states of consciousness by using psychotropic drugs and entering a sensory deprivation tank.

(851) The Predalien hybrid in the film Aliens vs Predator: Requiem was nicknamed "Chet" on set and in the script. This was to avoid early spoilers about the nature of the creature. Chet is a reference from the John Hughes film Weird Science.

(852) 2007 saw a terrible film called Chicago Massacre: Richard Speck come out. Speck was played by Corin Nemec - who had already played Ted Bundy in another forgettable serial killer biopic. Richard Speck was infamous for the torture and murder of eight student nurses from South Chicago Community Hospital in July 1966. Speck went into a student nursing dormitory and tied the women up. He raped, tortured, and killed them. One nurse survived by hiding under a bed. Speck was already known to the police for thirty previous arrests. He was known as a thief who robbed people at knifepoint. Speck claimed to be intoxicated on drugs when he murdered the nurses. The 1983 Charles Bronson action thriller film 10 to Midnight also seems to have been inspired by Richard Speck (and Ted Bundy too).

(853) The fantasy anthology series The Twilight Zone is one of the most famous and iconic shows in American television history. The show ended in 1964 and its creator Rod Serling sadly died far too young in 1975. In the early 1980s, Steven Spielberg (red hot at the time thanks to Raiders of the Lost Ark and E.T.) decided to make a big screen anthology version of The Twilight Zone and hired Joe Dante and George Miller to direct segments. The other two segments would be directed by Spielberg and his friend John Landis. Thanks to films like Animal House and An American Werewolf in London, Landis was one of the hottest young directors in Hollywood. Spielberg and Landis were such good friends that Spielberg even made a cameo in The Blues Brothers for Landis. The Twilight Zone movie was something of a vanity project for Landis and Spielberg and they couldn't wait to get started. They both loved The Twilight Zone and relished the chance to bring it to the big screen. Spielberg planned to direct a remake of The Monsters Are Due On Maple Street for the movie while Dante and Miller were also assigned classic TV episodes to update. Landis, eager to outdo the others, decided to come up with an original story called Time Out. The story was about a racist bigot who must experience persecution at the sharp end when he is sent back in time to Nazi Europe and Vietnam. Landis cast the actor Vic Morrow as the lead of his segment Time Out.

Morrow, now in his fifties, was best known for the old TV show Combat! but his career was rather in the doldrums by 1982. Morrow naturally jumped at the unexpected chance to be in a big movie like The Twilight Zone and thought this could resurrect his career. Little did he know though that the movie would actually cost him his life in horrendous fashion. The Twilight Zone film was completely overshadowed by a horrific helicopter accident on the set which killed Vic Morrow and two child extras (Renee Chen and My-ca Dinh Le) during the shooting of the John Landis contribution Time Out. Landis and his team had secretly paid the families of the child extras under the table and then used the children on a dangerous night shoot (this was all in violation of California's child labor laws). During a sequence set in war torn Vietnam, Vic Morrow was required to carry the two child extras across a wind machine lashed river as explosions went off around them and a helicopter loomed overhead. Morrow (who was no spring chicken) and the child extras should not have been doing this dangerous stunt. As the helicopter hovered into the shot, Landis kept shouting for the helicopter to get lower. Tragedy struck when the rotor blade was hit by debris from one of the explosions and the pilot lost control. The chopper violently and suddenly flipped over into the river and landed right on top of Morrow and the child actors. The children were killed instantly and Vic Morrow was decapitated by the rotor blade. A member of the crew later found Morrow's head floating in the river. This was probably the most gruesome and upsetting accident in Hollywood history. It was made all the worse by the fact that two of the victims were innocent children.

The tragic accident swiftly ended the friendship between Twilight Zone's producer Steven Spielberg (who not present on the set that night and devastated and angry when he found out what had happened - it's a pity Spielberg wasn't on the set because there is no way he would have permitted Landis to be so reckless)) and John Landis and led to a ten year manslaughter case in the courts. To the surprise of most observers, Landis somehow managed to evade any serious charges for the accident - despite the fact that he had needlessly put his lead actor and two child extras at risk simply because of his determination to capture a great shot for his film. Two books were written about the Twilight Zone accident and they both painted John Landis as a bombastic, reckless, and dangerous egomaniac. According to the book Outrageous Conduct, Landis even used live ammunition on the set of Time Out because he wanted it to look more realistic when plants and trees were shot up during the Vietnam segment.

(854) Neve Campbell has a somewhat less prominent role in Scream 3 because she was also shooting the TV show Party of Five at the same time.

(855) The basis of A Nightmare On Elm Street was inspired by several newspaper articles printed in the LA Times in the 1970s on a group of Southeast Asian refugees, who, after fleeing to the United States from the results of war and genocide in Laos, Cambodia, and Vietnam, were suffering disturbing nightmares, after which they refused to sleep. Some of the men died in their sleep soon after. Medical authorities called the phenomenon Asian Death Syndrome.

(856) The Rocky Horror Picture Show is a 1975 British musical film based on a stage production by Richard O'Brien and was directed by Jim Sharman. It created little fuss upon its initial release but subsequently became a cultural phenomenon when audiences/fans began turning up to repeat screenings, singing along to the musical numbers and even dressing up as the characters.

(857) Steven Spielberg was making Schindler's List while Jurassic Park was in post-production and he said he found it difficult and jarring to go back and forth from his harrowing holocaust drama to overseeing special effects for a dinosaur adventure film. It was a case of tonal whiplash to say the least.

(858) Edwin Neal, who plays the hitchhiker, said making The Texas Chainsaw Massacre was worse than his time in Vietnam during the war. Neal declined to appear in the sequel because he felt his proposed fee was an insult.

(859) Richard Attenborough played John Christie in the grim but compelling 1971 film 10 Rillington Place. John Christie was born in Yorkshire in 1899. Christie murdered at least eight people in London in the 1940s and 1950s - mostly by use of domestic gas. Once they were unconscious he would rape and then murder the victims. Christie served in the First World War but a gas attack left him unable to speak above a whisper. This made him seem like a very quiet and gentle man to people who met him but nothing could be further from the truth. Christie was quiet but he was certainly not gentle. He was married in the 1920s but soon separated from his wife. While

working as a postman, Christie stole some postal orders and got into trouble. He was a very untrustworthy man who was always tempted by a chance to make some money. Christie ended up in prison when he attacked a woman he was living with. He had apparently hit this poor woman over the head with a cricket bat. Christie later served another prison sentence for trying to steal a car. In the 1930s, Christie reconciled with his wife and moved to a flat at 10 Rillington Place. This address would become very famous in true crime lore thanks to Christie.

The flat was in Notting Hill but in those days the area was a lot more working-class and kitchen sink than it is today and definitely not the sort of place that Richard Curtis and Hugh Grant would hang around dispensing bon mots. John Christie's flat was on the top level of a house and the conditions were primitive and spartan. The shared toilet was outside and you were liable to freeze to death if you had to use it in the winter. During World War 2, Christie served as a reserve constable with the police. It was in the last few years of the war that his killing spree began. His first victim was Ruth Fuerst - a 21 year-old munitions worker. Fuerst was from Austria and it is believed she was supplementing her income by working as a prostitute in London. Christie throttled her and buried Fuerst in the back garden. Christie's second victim was Muriel Amelia Eady. Christie had a ruse where he would pose as someone with medical expertise. As this was before the days of the NHS (National Health Service), doctors were naturally difficult for those with no money to consult. Christie told Eady that he would cure her bronchitis. What he did instead was knock her out with domestic gas and then rape and strangle her. Once again, he buried the body in the back garden.

A few years later there was a tragic occurrence when a young woman named Beryl and her daughter were found dead in the outside toilet at Rillington Place. There was also a dead foetus. Beryl's husband Timothy Evans was arrested for the murders but he insisted he had nothing to do with it. Evans claimed

that Christie had offered to perform an abortion and then
killed them themselves. In what was clearly a miscarriage of
justice, Evans was convicted for the murders and hanged at
Pentonville Prison in 1950. John Christie had given evidence
in court against Evans and you can only imagine how
frustrating this must have been for Timothy Evans. He must
have felt like leaping across the court and strangling him.
Christie was a very cold and calculating man. It was later
established that the police had fabricated some evidence to
convict Evans. The fact that Christie served in the police
during the war patently made him seem more credible to
them. Christie's killing spree continued into the 1950s. In
1952, Christie murdered his wife so that he could have her
bank savings. In 1953 he murdered three women by use of gas
while they sat in the kitchen. The women were Kathleen
Maloney, Rita Nelson, and Hectorina MacLennan. Nelson was
pregnant at the time. Once the women were unconscious,
Christie strangled them with rope and stuffed the bodies in an
alcove.

The bodies of these last three victims were discovered by
another tenant in the house and John Christie was eventually
arrested by the police near Putney Bridge. Christie gave a full
confession and was put on trial. Christie was hanged on 15
July 1953 at Pentonville Prison. He was hung by the same
hangman who executed Timothy Evans. Rillington Place had
its named changed to Ruston Close after the grisly exploits of
John Christie came to light. In 1970, the street was demolished
to make way for new housing.

(860) George Romero and Stephen King's Creepshow is a
tribute to the infamous EC Horror Comics that both King and
Romero were heavily influenced by|when growing up and
features tales consisting (mostly) of various nasty people
getting their comeuppance in the compendium tradition. The
EC horror comics offered macabre morality tales in lurid
colour with all manner of deaths, monsters, zombies, murders
and general gruesome shenanigans until parents began to
notice what their children were reading and the comics were

banned. Romero and King both loved EC as children and came together to produce the ultimate - though of course unofficial - tribute to their childhood favourite.

(861) It was Sigourney weaver who insisted on there being no guns in Alien 3.

(862) Sterling Hayden was the first choice to play eccentric shark hunter Quint in Jaws. Hayden wasn't interested though and passed on the offer.

(863) Believe it or not, Tobe Hooper tried to get a PG rating for The Texas Chainsaw Massacre because he argued it was a suggestive horror film rather than an overtly explicit one.

(864) Guillermo Del Toro was offered the chance to direct Alien vs Predator but turned it down because he was busy developing Hellboy.

(865) Robert Rodriguez said he wanted to ignore Predator 2 and have Predators as the true sequel to Predator. This statement rather backfired as many people (including myself) think Predator 2 is much better than Predators.

(866) What happened to Damien: Omen II's young lead Jonathan Scott-Taylor? He seemed to vanish without trace in the 1980s. Information on Scott-Taylor is sketchy but there have been reports that he became a lawyer and started a business in Australia.

(867) Before Ridley Scott was hired, Steven Spielberg had some vague discussions about directing Alien. A clash of schedules (at the time Spielberg was due to make the comedy film 1941) meant that the discussions didn't get very far in the end.

(868) Freddy Krueger's appearance was inspired by a scary looking hobo that Wes Craven encountered as a child.

(869) Poltergeist was conceived by Steven Spielberg but although he wrote and produced the film he couldn't direct it because he was doing E.T.

(870) The little boy named Billy who features in the prologue to George Romero's Creepshow is played by Stephen King's son Joe.

(871) Stephen King said that Annie Wilkes in Misery was a metaphor for his drug addiction.

(872) IT Chapter 2 used 4,500 gallons of fake blood.

(873) The original plan in the Final Destination franchise was to have death as an entity or figure. This was changed to making death more vague and mysterious and presented by something as simple as a breeze blowing through a house.

(874) Psycho II was directed by Richard Franklin and written by Tom Holland. Although Robert Bloch wrote a sequel novel this film is more of an original piece. It sounds completely insane to make a sequel to Psycho decades later without the late Alfred Hitchcock but this confounded all expectations and turned out to be a very good thriller.

(875) In the 1981 horror sequel Halloween II a kid seems to be wearing a Michael Myers Halloween costume. How is this possible? Has Michael become an overnight celebrity?!

(876) Simon Pegg was offered the role of Spoon in Neil Marshall's Dog Soldiers but was about to make Shaun of the Dead and so declined.

(877) The burly man that Jeff Goldblum injures in the bar-room arm wrestling match in the 1986 remake of The Fly is George Chuvalo. Chuvalo was a rock chinned Canadian heavyweight boxer who fought Muhammad Ali twice.

(878) Nancy Allen and John Travolta had no idea they were

playing villains during production of the film version of Stephen King's Carrie. They were giving what they thought were comedic performances as shallow high school tropes.

(879) Texas Chainsaw 3D was directed by John Luessenhop. It is the seventh entry in the Texas Chainsaw series (which is a rather loose collection of sequels, reboots, remakes, and prequels). All you need to know about the Texas Chainsaw films is that the only ones worth watching are the first two. If you encounter one that wasn't directed by the great Tobe Hopper then run for the hills. Texas Chainsaw 3D begins as a mini-sequel to the first film and then spins off to do its own thing. The film starts after the events of the original The Texas Chainsaw Massacre. The townsfolk of Newt, Texas want revenge on the cannibal killers the Sawyer family and burn their house to the ground. All are killed save for a baby girl who is taken in by a local and his wife and raised as their own. The girl, now known as Heather (Alexandra Daddario), becomes a teenager and recieves a letter that her grandmother has died. She travels to the town of Newt with some friends to investigate her inheritance and - wouldn't you know it - soon finds out that she seems to be related to Leatherface, who turns out to be very much alive.

Texas Chainsaw 3D's mildly interesting prologue soon makes way for a depressingly run of the mill teen slasher with variable acting and no sense of atmosphere. Heather's friends are bumped off by Leatherface, who has been hiding in the house all this time, and the film inevitably moves towards Heather and Leatherface learning about one another with a predictable twist in the tale. Texas Chainsaw 3D is very substandard, even when placed against the disparate and mediocre collection of films that have traded on the good name of the original classic film. Tobe Hopper's sequel is worth watching but even that couldn't live up to the original so what chance did these later offspring have? Texas Chainsaw 3D is not only a bland forgettable horror film, it's also a stupid one. The action seems to be set in the present day and yet Heather only seems to be in her early twenties. If she was a baby during the events of the first film wouldn't she much older than that?

(880) There's a big subtext in Tobe Hooper's The Texas Chainsaw Massacre which many people miss. The Texas Chainsaw Massacre is a pro-Vegetarian film. In the film, humans are treated like animals. They are killed with hammers, hung on hooks, and turned into food. This gives us an insight into how horrific the meat industry is and how repellent human treatment of animals is. We don't need to kill animals for food but this cruel and hideous industry continues nonetheless. Making the film turned Tobe Hooper into a vegetarian.

(881) Phantasm is a cult 1979 low-budget horror film written and directed by Don Coscarelli. The story is set in a small Californian town (where people have started to vanish and dead bodies are mysteriously disappearing from the local cemetery) and revolves around perceptive shaggy haired adolescent Mike (Michael Baldwin) who lives with his older brother Jody (Bill Thornbury) after the death of their parents. Jody is a musician and plays together in a blues band with part-time ice cream man Reggie (Reggie Bannister) and Tommy (Bill Cone). Bad things start to happen though when Tommy is murdered in Morningside cemetery by a strange 'lady in lavender' (Kathy Lester) and young Mike surreptitiously tags along to attend the funeral. He is perturbed by some very odd noises and shocked to secretly spy the director of Morningside cemetery, a sinister and mysterious figure known as The Tall Man (Angus Scrimm), effortlessly lift Tommy's heavy coffin into a hearse single-handedly as if it weighed nothing at all.

The film is perhaps most famous for the strange flying metallic silver spheres that The Tall Man controls telepathically and uses to despatch people who poke their nose around the mausoleum too much for his liking. Coscarelli makes inventive use of these spheres with an eerie humming noise signalling their imminent arrival and plenty of fun low-angle camera shots from the POV of a sphere as it races towards someone down a corridor. The amazing mortuary sets (all accomplished on a shoestring budget) are a big part of the film and its strong undercurrent of dread and otherworldliness.

(882) Dick Van Dyke turned down the part of Robert Thorn in The Omen and later said he should have taken the part. Van Dyke was uneasy about appearing in a horror film because of his status as a family entertainer.

(883) One question that fans of John Carpenter's The Thing debate is whether or not Childs is the Thing when he and MacReady are left alone at the end. The argument for the theory that Childs is an alien is that he has no icy breath and MacReady laughs when Childs drinks from a bottle which may be a molotov cocktail. However, careful examination shows that Childs does have some ice breath earlier and that MacReady was about to drink from the bottle himself just before Childs arrived. The ending seems to be ambiguous.

(884) William Goldman says that it was incredibly difficult to get anyone to take the role of the kidnapped author in Rob Reiner's adaptation of Stephen King's Misery. James Caan was practically the last person they approached and had to take a drug test to prove he was fit and able to do it. Kevin Kline, Michael Douglas, Harrison Ford, Dustin Hoffman, Robert De Niro, Al Pacino, Richard Dreyfuss, Gene Hackman, and Robert Redford had all said no to the role of Paul Sheldon. Redford apparently expressed a mild interest but the producers didn't like the fact that he suggested changes to the script. Redford wanted to make the captive writer Paul less passive and less of a victim. That approach would appear to completely miss the point of the story.

(885) You might well have seen some of Victor Salva's films as he directed the three pictures in the Jeepers Creepers horror series. He was a protege of Francis Ford Coppola but his career was forever blighted during production on his 1988 film Clownhouse. Salva was convicted of sexual misconduct with

the then 12-year-old Nathan Winters, one of Clownhouse's underage stars including videotaping one of the encounters. Commercial videotapes and magazines containing child pornography were also found at his home. Salva pleaded guilty to lewd and lascivious conduct, oral sex with a person under 14, and procuring a child for pornography. He was sentenced to three years in state prison, of which he served 15 months. He completed his parole in 1992. It seems strange that Salva managed to continue his career but he has - in a fashion, with straight to DVD entries of late. There were demonstrations by his victim when 1995's Powder was released, a Disney film directed by Salva. The studio were understandably nervous and irritated when it dawned on them that they'd hired a convicted child molester. The Jeepers Creepers films were popular and entertaining although, given Salva's past, it was impossible to ignore his camera's particular fascination with teenage boys in the sequel. When Salva sent out a casting call for young teenagers to star in Jeepers Creepers 3 his ad was removed after people complained. It seems as if Salva will never be able to outrun his shameful past.

(886) The cult 1958 horror film The Fly was shot in just eighteen days.

(887) The Black Sisters in Harry Potter were probably inspired by the real life Mitford Sisters Unity and Diana. The Mitfords were from an aristocratic English family of socialites and became notorious for their support of fascism. Unity Mitford worshipped Adolf Hitler while Diana Mitford married British fascist leader Oswald Mosley.

(888) Xtro is a cultishly bizarre 1982 sci-fi horror film directed by Harry Bromley Davenport. A man is kidnapped by a UFO and three years later returns (a woman gives birth to him fully grown in a famously disgusting scene) to be with his son and estranged wife but - naturally - he isn't quite the man that he used to be. Xtro is often jumbled in with Alien clones thanks to the birth scene and a few moments of extraterrestial horror (the alien creature seen in the road by the woods at night is

rather creepy) but, generally, there aren't a huge amount of similarities despite this often appearing on lists of films that were inspired by Alien. The most obvious Alien homages are a facehugger (of sorts) in one of the endings and alien eggs. Xtro is really only for those who enjoy surreal and strange low-budget horror films. Not an awful lot makes any sense here and the director Harry Bromley Davenport has candidly admitted in interviews that Xtro was never meant to have narrative logic or any coherence. They were more or less making it up as they went along. It was merely meant to be disgusting and make some money (and succeeded on both of those counts)

(889) Jeff Bridges, Christopher Walken, Nick Nolte, Kris Kristofferson and Sam Shepard were considered for the part of MacReady in John Carpenter's The Thing.

(890) The Evil Dead was caught up in the 1980s 'video nasty' hysteria in Britain and banned for a time. It seems as if the film's sense of humour was lost on the BBFC (British Board of Film Classification).

(891) Bette Midler turned down the part of Annie Wilkes in the film version of Misery.

(892) It's Dan O'Herlihy who steals the show in Halloween III as the wicked toymaker Cochran. O'Herlihy really seems to be enjoying himself as the villain here. Watch for his barely disguised contempt when he shows the doomed salesman and his family around the factory. It's a great performance.

(893) Believe it or not there is a horror film called Dahmer vs. Gacy where these two notorious serial killers are cloned, get loose, and do battle. Though played for laughs, Dahmer vs. Gacy is strictly bottom of the barrel amateur hour and best avoided.

(894) Xtro II: The Second Encounter is 1990 sequel to (the mildly cultish) Xtro and had Harry Bromley Davenport back in

the director's chair. Davenport only made the film though because he needed the money. This one has no connection to the original Xtro and was made in Canada (as opposed to the original which was a British film). They look as if they spent even less money on this one than Xtro. At least in the original they had some outdoor location work. Xtro II is a rip-off of both Alien and James Cameron's Aliens. The film is set in an underground government research base where experiments into other dimensions take place. When a creature from another dimension becomes at large in the base a group of soldiers and scientists must fight for survival. Xtro II is a very bargain basement Aliens but also references Alien. Yet again in one of these Alien franchise clones we get creature bursting from someone's chest at the start.

 Xtro II is another of those cheap science fiction horror films that sounds a lot more entertaining on paper than it actually is to watch. The entire film takes place in what looks like a warehouse and you only see the alien creature a few times (it is slimy and vaguely Gigeresque). Xtro II is always battling its non existent budget and the lack of money ultimately sinks the film. Well, that and some truly atrocious acting from the cast. The only famous name on offer is Airwolf star Jan Michael Vincent. Vincent genuinely looks as if he has no idea what he's doing in this film. He barely looks as if he's awake and his disinterest is all too apparent. Harry Bromley Davenport later said that he had to read out the lines to Vincent before each scene because the actor never bothered to read the script. Watching the film and Jan Michael Vincent's performance, that news doesn't come as a huge surprise. Xtro II is a scraping from the bottom of the barrel as far as Alien franchise rip-off films go and never offers sufficient horror or action to keep the viewer interested. Ultimately, the clear absence of any budget completely torpedoes the film.

(896) In 1995, Harry Bromley Davenport decided the world was ready for yet more Xtro capers and released Xtro 3: Watch the Skies. This is slightly more watchable than Xtro II but that's not exactly a big achievement. The story in this one has a

squad of marines trapped on an island with a vengeful alien who was captured and experimented on at a secret facility. There are riffs on Alien and Aliens but the film that Xtro 3 rips off the most is Predator. As with the first Xtro sequel, Harry Bromley Davenport is hamstrung by a miniscule budget (you have to wait forever for any action in this film and even when it does arrive it seems small scale and inept) and an amatuerish cast who bark at each other and give embarrassing performances. There is though a cameo by Robert Culp as an army general. How on earth did they persuade Robert Culp to appear in this? They must have blown half the budget on his fee. Xtro 3 is largely a waste of time (save perhaps for a slightly surreal sequence when they stumble across some alien technology conveyed by lights and laser beams) and only for curious Xtro completists (if there is such a thing).

(897) When he made Phantasm II, Don Coscarelli was given a larger than usual budget (by Universal in this case) but it seems the studio had the final say in casting. So, Michael Baldwin, who plays Mike in all the other Phantasm films, is replaced in this one by the goofily handsome James LeGros. At least he managed to keep Reggie Bannister although, unbelievably, Reggie had to audition to reprise his part!

(898) 1987's dreadful Jaws: The Revenge begs a salient question. Why doesn't Ellen Brody just move to a landlocked country? Move to Switzerland!

(899) The original Invasion of the Body Snatchers had a fifties small town setting but the excellent 1978 version interestingly switches the action to a large city - where of course it would actually be far more difficult to tell who is a pod person or acting weirdly!

(900) The Monster Squad is a cult 1987 comedy horror adventure film directed by Fred Dekker. Dekker also wrote the screenplay with Shane Black. If you love Stranger Things you should enjoy this film. The story begins with a Transylvania prologue set in 1887. At a spooky castle, Dr Van Helsing (Jack

Gwillim) attempts to banish Count Dracula (Duncan Regehr) into limbo on the "day of balance" between good and evil. This is only possible once every century and an indestructible shimmering green amulet of concentrated good must be at hand. Are you following this so far? Anyway, Van Helsing "blew it" (as the irreverent text scroll at the start of the film tells us) and Dracula resurfaces one hundred years later in 1987. The amulet was hidden far away in a small American town by Van Helsing's associates and the Count arrives to claim it and so plunge the world into darkness. To this end he puts together a team of classic Universal studio monsters to help him. Frankenstein's Monster (Tom Noonan), The Mummy (Michael MacKay), The Gill-Man aka Creature from the Black Lagoon (Tom Woodruff Jr), and The Wolf Man (Carl Thibault). The only thing that stands in their way is a bunch of plucky monster obsessed kids with a treehouse who call themselves The Monster Squad. This film seemed to slip through a portal into limbo itself but seems to be getting the love it deserves now.

(901) The supermarket in Shaun of the Dead is called Landis in tribute to John Landis.

(902) 1953's Robot Monster was directed by Phil Tucker and written by Wyott Ordung. Earth has been attacked by aliens, chiefly Ro-Man (George Barrows) - who looks like a man in a gorilla costume wearing a deep sea diving helmet with TV aerials. Ro-Man has killed everyone on Earth with a Calcinator death ray. But not so fast. A few humans have apparently survived. The survivors are a scientist (John Mylong), his wife (Selena Royle), and their family. Robot Monster is a famously bad film but it's quite charming in its own ridiculous way. This is one of those films that can't help but make you smile and give you a preposterous hour of entertainment. Ro-Man is a completely pathetic villain in that he can't even seem to dispense with a family of survivors in a quarry and spends much of his time lumbering around in a cave with what looks like a bubble machine. Even the kids mock him when they come face to face. The hand gestures of Barrows seldom seem

to match Ro-Man's dialogue and this supplies a lot of comedy (which probably wasn't intended). The strange thing about Robot Monster is that the actors playing the family are delivering fairly straight (if hardly Oscar winning) performances.

(903) Cat People is a 1942 horror film produced by Val Lewton and directed by Jacques Tourneur. DeWitt Bodeen wrote the original screenplay - which was based on Val Lewton's short story The Bagheeta. Serbian émigré Irena Dubrovna (Simone Simon) attracts the attention of marine engineer Oliver Reed (Kent Smith) at the zoo after she discards some paper on which she was sketching a black panther. The pair have some tea together and become close - eventually marrying. However, Irene believes that she is cursed because of witchcraft in her old European village and that if she becomes intimate with her husband she will turn into a panther and place him in great harm.

This film noir horror film is justifiably famous and richly atmospheric. It is famously credited with inventing a technique where the audience is led to believe that something dramatic or frightening is about to happen but then have that undercut by a moment that dissipates the tension but makes them jump at the same time. In the film, there is a scene where Alice is followed down a dark street at night by what she thinks is a big cat predator and just as the growls seem to heighten and she seems to be in imminent danger, a bus suddenly pulls into shot from nowhere with the brakes squealing loudly like a high pitched animal sound. The bus makes us jump. It's like a false jump scare. This technique was forever known as the Lewton bus.

(904) Phoebe Cates' famous speech in Gremlins about why she hates Christmas was not liked by either the studio or producer Steven Spielberg but director Joe Dante fought his corner and kept it in the film.

(905) At an early stage of its development, Scream 2 was going

to be called Scream Again, Scream Louder.

(906) The Dark Half was directed by George Romero and adapted from Stephen King's novel. The premise was inspired by Stephen King's own pseudonym Richard Bachman. King wrote several novels under the Bachman name as an experiment when he became concerned that his books were selling mainly because they had his name on the front cover. When he was rumbled by a journalist, King buried Bachman just as Thad buries Stark and he used the experience for the basis of The Dark Half.

(907) The Shining is incredibly rich in atmosphere and a foreboding sense of dread and Kubrick does a fantastic job in designing and creating the hotel. The exteriors at the beginning of the film (taken from the original ending to Blade Runner) were shot in Colorado - the wonderful opening image of the Torrance car winding its way around the mountain roads from high above. Exteriors were shot at Elstree in Britain and great care is taken to make the hotel as strange and labyrinth as possible. A place where you really could lose your mind if you were not careful.

(908) John Carpenter said he wasn't terribly enthused about adapting Stephen King's Christine for the screen but he had to do the film because he needed a job after The Thing bombed at the box-office. Carpenter said he was happy at the way the film turned out though and it turned out to be a much better experience than he had anticipated.

(909) Doug Bradley said he gave the film critic Barry Norman quite a scare when he bumped into him by chance in full Pinhead costume on the set of Hellraiser II.

(910) Carrie Henn was chosen from 500 children to play "Newt" in Aliens.

(911) Despite having a running time of 127 minutes, Jurassic Park only contains 15 minutes of actual dinosaur action.

(912) A slightly bizarre piece of Predator trivia is that two members of the cast (Arnold Schwarzenegger, Jessie Ventura) went into politics and became Governors. Sonny Landham tried (and failed) to make it a hat trick when he ran in the Republican Party primary election for the post of Governor of Kentucky.

(913) After many actors turned the part down, the two main candidates at one point for the part of MacReady in John Carpenter's The Thing were Tom Atkins and Jack Thompson. Carpenter ultimately decided to go for Kurt Russell - whom he'd worked with on Elvis and Escape from New York.

(914) From conception to post-production, Stanley Kubrick took five years to finish The Shining.

(915) John Hurt was the first choice to play Kane in Alien but already contracted to make Zulu Dawn in South Africa. Jon Finch was cast instead but suffered a severe diabetic episode when shooting began and had to drop out. John Hurt met with Ridley Scott and agreed to to replace Finch. Hurt began shooting his scenes the next morning. Believe it or not, Hurt was only available because he had been banned from South Africa after being mistaken for John Heard - an anti-Apartheid campaigner!

(916) Ridley Scott's 2003 director's cut of Alien adds the scenes where Ripley finds the cocooned bodies of two crew members near the end of the film.

(917) The 1981 horror film Wolfen film was the first to use a thermographic visual photographic look to represent the point-of-view of a character. This POV device was later used famously in Predator.

(918) Denise Nickerson, famous as Violet Beauregarde in 1971's Willy Wonka & the Chocolate Factory, was in the frame to play Regan MacNeil in The Exorcist but her parents

objected to the material and wouldn't let her become a serious candidate.

(919) Miracle Mile, an apocalyptic thriller screenplay by Steve De Jarnatt later turned into an unappreciated 1988 film, was at one point going to be used as the basis for Twilight Zone: The Movie until they decided to use the anthology format instead. If they had adapted Miracle Mile rather than having different segments then the dreadful helicopter accident involving Vic Morrow would not have occurred. A very bitter twist of fate.

(920) It was deemed too dangerous to film in real caves for Neil Marshall's excellent horror film The Descent so cave sets were built at Pinewood Studios.

(921) Michael Keaton turned down the lead role in the 1986 remake of The Fly.

(922) The Wicker Man was shot in Gatehouse of Fleet, Newton Stewart, Kirkcudbright and a few scenes in the village of Creetown in Dumfries and Galloway, as well as Plockton in Ross-shire. Britt Ekland had to apologise after calling Galloway the bleakest place on earth.

(923) One of the working titles for Night of the Living Dead was Night of the Flesh Eaters.

(924) Although we think of Aliens as a big film it was made on a limited budget (under $20 million) and the crew had to improvise. The APC that ferries the marines around was a vehicle used to pull jumbo jets at airports but modified to look more like a military carrier. Part of Ripley's apartment at Gateway station is a modified British Airways toilet.

(925) The scene where Damien speaks to his satanic followers in Omen III was shot at a quarry with 450 extras.

(926) In 1987's Predator, Shane Black plays Hawkins, the

commando team's bespectacled radio operator. Black was a screenwriter and had recently written Lethal Weapon and The Monster Squad at the time. Black was shrewdly given a supporting actor role in the film by 20th Century Fox so they would have someone at the heart of the production to keep an eye on the inexperienced director John McTiernan and the script.

(927) Note how Jay swims in her garden at the start of It Follows as if it is summer and then goes out later on and everyone is dressed in winter coats. This jumble of time gives the film a nicely off-kilter feel.

(928) Despite playing Pennywise in a famous television miniseries version of Stephen King's IT, Tim Curry said he is scared of clowns!

(929) Linnea Quigley's character in Return of the Living Dead was originally going to be called Legs but was later changed to Trash.

(930) John Carpenter's inspiration for his film The Fog was a visit to a fog shrouded Stonehenge.

(931) The spaceship uniforms in Galaxy of Terror came from the recently cancelled Battlestar Galactica television show.

(932) Lee Van Cleef and Jerry Ohrbach were considered for the part of Gary played by Donald Moffat in John Carpenter's The Thing.

(933) Tobe Hooper feels that the black comedy in The Texas Chainsaw Massacre was missed by many critics. Note how the Sawyer cannibal clan are like a pastiche of an all American family with the cook as the cranky dad, the hitchhiker as the wayward teen, Leatherface as the mother figure.

(934) New Zealand filmmaker Geoff Murphy was the original director of 1987's Predator. Murphy said he was fired because

he disagreed with the choice of Arnold Schwarzenegger as the lead.

(935) The entertaining and blood drenched 2016 killer clown film Terrifier was made for just $35,0000.

(936) The original Saw movie was intended to be a straight to DVD release but turned out to be a (highly successful) theatrical film.

(937) John Carpenter's Halloween was shot during the summer. They had to put paper leaves on the ground to make it seem like Autumn.

(938) The early concept for Alien was that the characters would find a strange pyramid on the nightmare planet. This concept was later used in Alien v Predator.

(939) Hammer were interested in remaking King Kong in the late sixties ad early seventies and had some meetings with RKO to discuss this. In the end though they didn't get the rights or go ahead with with this. Not much is known about Hammer's plans but it is speculated that they might have set the film in the Victorian period.

(940) Richard Johnson, the lead actor in the classic horror film The Haunting, was chosen by director Terence Young to be the first ever James Bond in Dr No. Johnson didn't want to be tied to a multi-film contract though and passed on the offer - thus paving the way for Sean Connery to become Bond.

(941) Akira is a Japanese manga and animation. It takes place in a futuristic Neo-Tokyo in 2019 that has been rebuilt after the city was destroyed. Tetsuo is a member of a biker gang who develops growing psychic powers after an encounter with a child. As the powers develop, and Tetsuo begins to become unhinged, he attracts the attention of a secret government project directed by JSDF Colonel Shikishima.

(942) The Boston Strangler case involved 13 women (of varying ages) being murdered in Boston between 1962 and 1964. The killer used a nylon stocking to strangle many of his victims. Albert DeSalvo was convicted for the Boston Strangler murders. DeSalvo may have raped as many as 300 women and confessed to the Strangler killings. There are those though who feel the murders were too eclectic in nature to have all been carried out by one man. Tony Curtis played Albert DeSalvo in a film based on the Boston Strangler case. The movie version of this notorious case is well regarded and worth watching.

(943) George Romero was born in New York in 1940 and began making films as a child with his uncle's 8mm camera. In 1957 he moved to Pittsburgh to study commercial art but was soon drawn back to filmmaking, working as a runner on Hitchcock's North By Northwest and dropping out of college to start a commercials business.

(944) A Clockwork Orange was released in 1971 and adapted by Kubrick from the 1962 Anthony Burgess fable about the choice between good and evil. This is the most infamous of Kubrick's films because it was banned in Britain for many years - its mystique and notoriety of course reaching near legendary proportions because it was forbidden fruit and largely unseen in the country where it was made. The film provoked something of a media storm when it first appeared and was interpreted by some as a celebration of how great it is to be bad. When there were stories of copycat violence and a judge branded it a wicked film, Kubrick asked Warner Bros not to distribute the film in Britain anymore. He never really explained if he was genuinely disturbed by the effect the film might be having on some troubled souls or if he was just sick to death of all the attention. Maybe it was a combination of the two.

(945) John Cusack played Alaska wilderness serial killer Robert Hansen in the so-so 2013 film The Frozen Ground. Robert Hansen was born in Estherville, Iowa, in 1939. Robert Hansen was a killer most active in the 1970s. He moved to

Alaska where he opened a bakery. However, he had a very disturbing and sadistic hobby aside from baking. Hansen would kidnap women (many of whom were prostitutes or dancers from strip clubs) and then turn them loose in the wilderness so he could hunt them. He eventually confessed to thirteen murders. Some allege that Robert Hansen did not hunt his victims and that this was an embellishment that derived from him once having to chase one down after she escaped. There is no doubt though that he was a sick and ruthless man responsible for the deaths of many innocent people.

(946) The Exorcist was the first horror movie to be nominated for a Best Picture Oscar.

(947) Britt Ekland's character had a 'bottom' double for the famous scene in The Wicker Man where she knocks on Howie's door while naked. Eklund was annoyed about this because she refused to do waist down nudity but everyone presumed it was her in the film. They shot the scene when Eklund was not on the set so she knew nothing about it.

(948) The classic John Carpenter film Halloween is often credited with inventing the 'slasher' rule that the more promiscuous characters are bumped off - whereas the more virginal heroine is liable to survive. Carpenter said that this 'trope' had never occurred to him when they made Halloween and it was all purely accidental.

(949) Dementors, the deadly phantoms that guard Azkaban Prison in Harry Potter, represent depression and were based on JK Rowling's own experiences of the condition.

(950) Tim Burton was in line to direct Gremlins but producer Steven Spielberg ultimately felt it was too risky a choice as Burton had only directed animated shorts.

(951) For the famous chestburster scene in Alien, Ridley Scott did not tell the actors exactly what was going to happen to get

more of a natural reaction out of them. One can see that Veronica Cartwright as Lambert in particular looks genuinely horrified when the blood spurts up.

(952) A ludicrous 2006 Hollywood remake of The Wicker Man starring Nicholas Cage was panned by critics. This film is widely mocked on YouTube.

(953) The poster for the Texas Chainsaw Massacre 2 was a pastiche of the John Hughes teen drama film The Breakfast Club.

(954) The original Westworld was a 1973 science fiction thriller film written and directed by Michael Crichton. Crichton thought Westworld was a very visual concept and so would work better as a film than a book. Crichton found his first cut of the film dull so he radically trimmed it down to help the pace. Among the sequences deleted were a hovercraft scene and a bank raid.

(955) Sam Raimi only made Evil Dead II because his film Crimewave had bombed and he needed to make something that had a better chance of success.

(956) The studio making Jaws wanted Jan Michael Vincent to play Hooper. Steven Spielberg obviously wasn't convinced and cast Richard Dreyfuss instead.

(957) The voice making the robotic announcements in the mall ("Attention shoppers") in 1978's Dawn of the Dead is Christine Forrest (George Romero's wife).

(958) Ringu is a 1998 Japanese horror film directed by Hideo Nakata and adapted from the novel by Koji Suzuki. The film begins with an enjoyably spooky prologue of sorts as two teenage girls (Masami & Tomoko) lark about at home discussing an urban legend about a cursed videotape that everyone is talking about at school. The tape is said to kill anyone that watches it within seven days - with the victim

receiving a telephone call immediately after it ends to signal/confirm they are now to die. The jovial aura is punctured somewhat when Tomoko nervously reveals that, along with three of her friends, she watched this notorious videotape a week ago and then received the dreaded phone call. The girls soon discover that the curse is very real and a terrified Masami is witness to the death of Tomoko. Tomoko's aunt, reporter Asakawa Reiko (Nanako Matsushima), has already heard about the stories circulating of strange deaths amongst teenagers - they are found with their faces grotesquely frozen in fear - after interviewing some school children for a piece about urban legends. The death of her niece motivates her to investigate further and she discovers the three friends Tomoko watched the tape with all died on the same night as her and that Masami was so traumatised she ended up insane and in an institution. Asakawa works out that Tomoko and her friends stayed in a rental cabin in Izu and travels there, finding a copy of this notorious tape. She decides to view it for herself - and thus becomes cursed.

A nice touch in Ringu is that after Asakawa watches the tape we get a frequent reminder of the date onscreen to stress that she is running out of time to find the source of the mystery and save herself. This is something that The Amityville Horror also did and it's interesting that Ringu contains several moments that remind one of Hollywood horror films like Scream and Poltergeist. These influences are given a thoroughly Japanese twist and the end result is very effective and enjoyable. Ringu's most famous moment shares Poltergeist's obsession with a particular household staple and is certainly creepy.

(959) The script for the original Friday the 13th film was written in two weeks.

(960) Fulci's Restaurant in Shaun of the Dead is a reference to Italian horror director Lucio Fulci.

(961) William Friedkin called The Babadook the most terrifying film he had ever seen.

(962) Linda Blair received death threats after The Exorcist came out. Religious nuts are thought to be the culprits.

(963) David Walliams auditioned for the role played by Dylan Moran in Shaun of the Dead.

(964) John D Brown started directing Jaws 2 but was fired by the studio. Jeannot Szwarc replaced him. Brown's intended version of Jaws 2 was darker and more blood drenched. In Brown's aborted film, Amity is a ghost town and has never recovered from the shark hysteria of the first Jaws. The politicians decide to open the beaches again because they owe money to the Mafia. The film had been shooting for a month when executives pulled the plug. They didn't like the footage he'd shot.

(965) The working title of the film Predator was Hunter.

(966) V/H/S/2 arrived in 2013. The V/H/S sequel proves that less is sometimes more. It's no Dead of Night but the four stories are more memorable than the ones in the first film and the directing talent is better. The found footage is handled better too although one could be forgiven of being sick of found footage films by now. That's one niche that has been hammered to death.

(967) From a Whisper to a Scream is gruesome anthology from 1987 directed by Jeff Burr and also known as The Offspring. Vincent Price features in the wraparound and later regretted it apparently because he found the film distasteful. No one can deny that Burr goes for broke here. Necrophilia, cannibalism, incest, voodoo, deformities, and murderous children. It's a rather grim anthology but you can't fault it for effort. This is a twisted and sometimes brutal compendium.

(968) Despite being set in Scotland, the film Dog Soldiers was mostly shot in Luxembourg.

(969) Entertainment Weekly ranked The Omen as the 14th scariest film of all time.

(970) Virginia Madsen, the star of Candyman, is allergic to bees in real life.

(971) For the shower scene in Psycho, Hitchcock made the water cold so that Janet Leigh's screams would be more convincing.

(972) Vincent Price was offered the part of horror film actor Paul Henderson in The House THat Dripped Blood but had to decline because of a contract with American International Pictures. He was replaced by Jon Pertwee, an actor who had just become the third incarnation of Doctor Who on television.

(973) The Ford Pinto driven by Joyce Byers in Stranger Things is the same car used by the besieged family in the film adaptation of Stephen King's Cujo.

(974) The familiar trademarks and techniques of John Carpenter are empty rooms and streets (emptiness represents suspicion and generates anticipation), flawed Hawksian heroes we can sort of relate to, Pyrrhic victories, distrust of government and authority, electronic music with accentuating notes, a love of anamorphic Panavision, and minimal exposition when telling a story.

(975) The set for the town in Gremlins was also used for Twin Pines in Back to the Future.

(976) Linda Blair didn't want to go through the demon make-up again for Exorcist II: The Heretic so they used some flashbacks from the first film and even a different actress.

(977) Dr Terror's House of Horrors kick-started the Amicus series of British compendium horror films and was shot at Shepperton Studios with a budget of £105,000. Amicus creative chiefs Milton Subotsky and Max J Rosenberg decided

to take on rival Hammer by adopting the anthology structure of the classic 1945 Ealing film Dead of Night (the treatment for Dr Terror's House of Horrors apparently dated way back to the era just after Dead of Night). Subotsky had apparently submitted a Frankenstein script to Hammer before their success with the old Universal staples but the script was rejected and left him with a certain bitterness towards the famed horror studio.

(978) Vincent Price's daughter said that her father disliked the 'slasher' films which became popular in the seventies and eighties.

(979) Actor/co-producer Karl Hardman, who plays Harry Cooper in George Romero's Night of the Living Dead, also served as the makeup artist and electronic sound effects engineer

(980) Donald Pleasence only did Halloween because his daughter liked John Carpenter's Assault on Precinct 13.

(981) Milo Ventimiglia, Freddy Rodríguez and Josh Brolin were considered for the role of Royce in Predators.

(982) The cross-pollination of actresses between Hammer and the Bond series is unsurprising as both franchises were British based and required a regular influx of young model type women for their pictures.

(983) Sissy Spacek put grease in her hair and wore dirty clothes for her Carrie audition to dampen down a sense that she was too good looking to play the character.

(984) Michael Caine missed the Oscar ceremony (where he was up for his part in Woody Allen's Hannah and Her Sisters) because of reshoots on Jaws: The Revenge. Caine says he's never actually seen Jaws: The Revenge but did buy his mother a new house with the money he got paid to do it.

(985) Richard Chaves, who plays Poncho in Predator, was a real life Vietnam veteran.

(986) "Frankly, I feel like the grandfather of Alien," said Jerome Bixby, the writer of It! The Terror from Beyond Space. "There's a whole roster of similarities between what I wrote and Alien. They're both about a small group of people trapped aboard a spacecraft with an inimical creature out to get them and which, in fact, knocks them off one by one. No problem there; that's a pretty general plot outline. In both stories the creatures use the ship's air ducts. In both stories they are held off with gas and electricity. And at the end of both stories, they're dispatched by suffocation, by evacuating the creatures from the ship and depriving them of air." Bixby was philosophical about Alien borrowing from his film as he openly admitted that It! The Terror from Beyond Space was in turn heavily influenced by The Thing From Another World.

(987) Stephen King was frequently drunk and stoned when he directed the film Maximum Overdrive in the eighties. This was an adaption of one of King's stories and about trucks and cars coming to life and trying to run down people. Anyone who has ever watched some of this film will probably not be surprised to learn that King was a bit out of it at the time!

(988) George Romero's Living Dead series is about the complete domination of a materialist consumer culture where the living are every bit as mindless and uniform as the dead.

(989) Sam Raimi's Army of Darkness was unreleased for a year because of studio politics.

(990) The opening narration and documentary approach to the start of The Texas Chainsaw Massacre is designed to make it seem like the film is based on real events.

(991) Michael Myers wears a Captain Kirk Star Trek mask spray painted white in Halloween. John Carpenter joked that he owes his whole career to William Shatner!

(992) The Wicker Man was shot in October and so fake plastic blossoms had to be put on the trees to make it look like summer.

(993) Gunnar Hansen couldn't see clearly when he was wearing the Leatherface mask in Texas Chainsaw Massacre and nearly knocked himself out a few times.

(994) Black Christmas was the main inspiration for John Carpenter's Halloween.

(995) Firestarter is 1980 Stephen King novel, later turned into a 1984 film. Firestarter is about a little girl named Charlie with pyrokinetic abilities which she gained from her parents taking a hallucinogenic known as 'Lot 6' as part of experiments when they were in college. A secret government agency known as 'The Shop' wants to use Charlie as a weapon. The film was recently remade. Firestarter was a big influence on the television show Stranger Things.

(996) Peter Cushing said when he played Baron Frankenstein he would constantly ask his doctor about the correct way to remove a head or something so that he could do the scene as accurately as possible!

(997) James Horner's incredible score for Aliens is all the more remarkable with the knowledge that it was composed at the last minute against the clock.

(998) An early treatment for Texas Chainsaw Massacre 2 had Sally Hardesty's return to Texas to exact revenge on the murderous family - who are now running a hotel.

(999) Sherman Howard, who plays the domesticated zombie 'Bub' in Day of the Dead, has said that he doesn't think this film is very good. It hasn't stopped him attending numerous conventions to make money out of it though!

(1000) Martin Scorsese defended Exorcist II and said it was one of his guilty pleasures. Scorsese even said he prefers it to the original film!